Modern Critical Interpretations

Ernest Hemingway's
A Farewell to Arms

Modern Critical Interpretations

The Oresteia
Beowulf
The General Prologue to
  The Canterbury Tales
The Pardoner's Tale
The Knight's Tale
The Divine Comedy
Exodus
Genesis
The Gospels
The Iliad
The Book of Job
Volpone
Doctor Faustus
The Revelation of St.
  John the Divine
The Song of Songs
Oedipus Rex
The Aeneid
The Duchess of Malfi
Antony and Cleopatra
As You Like It
Coriolanus
Hamlet
Henry IV, Part I
Henry IV, Part II
Henry V
Julius Caesar
King Lear
Macbeth
Measure for Measure
The Merchant of Venice
A Midsummer Night's
  Dream
Much Ado About
  Nothing
Othello
Richard II
Richard III
The Sonnets
Taming of the Shrew
The Tempest
Twelfth Night
The Winter's Tale
Emma
Mansfield Park
Pride and Prejudice
The Life of Samuel
  Johnson
Moll Flanders
Robinson Crusoe
Tom Jones
The Beggar's Opera
Gray's Elegy
Paradise Lost
The Rape of the Lock
Tristram Shandy
Gulliver's Travels

Evelina
The Marriage of Heaven
  and Hell
Songs of Innocence and
  Experience
Jane Eyre
Wuthering Heights
Don Juan
The Rime of the Ancient
  Mariner
Bleak House
David Copperfield
Hard Times
A Tale of Two Cities
Middlemarch
The Mill on the Floss
Jude the Obscure
The Mayor of
  Casterbridge
The Return of the Native
Tess of the D'Urbervilles
The Odes of Keats
Frankenstein
Vanity Fair
Barchester Towers
The Prelude
The Red Badge of
  Courage
The Scarlet Letter
The Ambassadors
Daisy Miller, The Turn
  of the Screw, and
  Other Tales
The Portrait of a Lady
Billy Budd, Benito Cer-
  eno, Bartleby the Scriv-
  ener, and Other Tales
Moby-Dick
The Tales of Poe
Walden
Adventures of
  Huckleberry Finn
The Life of Frederick
  Douglass
Heart of Darkness
Lord Jim
Nostromo
A Passage to India
Dubliners
A Portrait of the Artist as
  a Young Man
Ulysses
Kim
The Rainbow
Sons and Lovers
Women in Love
1984
Major Barbara

Man and Superman
Pygmalion
St. Joan
The Playboy of the
  Western World
The Importance of Being
  Earnest
Mrs. Dalloway
To the Lighthouse
My Antonia
An American Tragedy
Murder in the Cathedral
The Waste Land
Absalom, Absalom!
Light in August
Sanctuary
The Sound and the Fury
The Great Gatsby
A Farewell to Arms
The Sun Also Rises
Arrowsmith
Lolita
The Iceman Cometh
Long Day's Journey Into
  Night
The Grapes of Wrath
Miss Lonelyhearts
The Glass Menagerie
A Streetcar Named
  Desire
Their Eyes Were
  Watching God
Native Son
Waiting for Godot
Herzog
All My Sons
Death of a Salesman
Gravity's Rainbow
All the King's Men
The Left Hand of
  Darkness
The Brothers Karamazov
Crime and Punishment
Madame Bovary
The Interpretation of
  Dreams
The Castle
The Metamorphosis
The Trial
Man's Fate
The Magic Mountain
Montaigne's Essays
Remembrance of Things
  Past
The Red and the Black
Anna Karenina
War and Peace

These and other titles in preparation

Modern Critical Interpretations

Ernest Hemingway's

A Farewell to Arms

Edited and with an introduction by
Harold Bloom
Sterling Professor of the Humanities
Yale University

Chelsea House Publishers
NEW YORK ◊ PHILADELPHIA

© 1987 by Chelsea House Publishers, a division
of Main Line Book Co.

Introduction © 1987 by Harold Bloom

Printed and bound in the United States of America

10   9   8   7   6   5   4

∞ The paper used in this publication meets the minimum
requirements of the American National Standard for Permanence
of Paper for Printed Library Materials, Z39.48–1984.

Library of Congress Cataloging-in-Publication Data
Ernest Hemingway's A farewell to arms.
    (Modern critical interpretations)
    Bibliography: p.
    Includes index.
    Contents: Introduction / Harold Bloom—The novel
as pure poetry / Daniel J. Schneider—Tragic form in
A farewell to arms / Robert Merrill—[etc.]
    1. Hemingway, Ernest, 1899–1961.   Farewell to arms.
2. World War, 1914–1918—Literature and the war.
[1. Hemingway, Ernest, 1899–1961.   Farewell to arms.
2. World War, 1914–1918—Literature and the war.
3. American literature—History and criticism]
I. Bloom, Harold.   II. Series.
PS3515.E37F7338   1987   813'.52   87–8056
ISBN 1–55546–044–5

Contents

Editor's Note / vii

Introduction / 1
    HAROLD BLOOM

The Novel as Pure Poetry / 9
    DANIEL J. SCHNEIDER

Tragic Form in *A Farewell to Arms* / 25
    ROBERT MERRILL

A Farewell to Arms: A Dream Book / 33
    WILLIAM ADAIR

Going Back / 49
    MICHAEL S. REYNOLDS

Hemingway's "Resentful Cryptogram" / 61
    JUDITH FETTERLEY

The Sense of an Ending in *A Farewell to Arms* / 77
    BERNARD OLDSEY

Frederic Henry's Escape and the Pose
of Passivity / 97
    SCOTT DONALDSON

Pseudoautobiography and Personal Metaphor / 113
    MILLICENT BELL

Catherine Barkley and the Hemingway Code: Ritual
and Survival in *A Farewell to Arms* / 131
    SANDRA WHIPPLE SPANIER

Chronology / 149

Contributors / 151

Bibliography / 153

Acknowledgments / 157

Index / 159

Editor's Note

This book gathers together a representative selection of the best criticism devoted to Ernest Hemingway's novel *A Farewell to Arms*. The critical essays are reprinted here in the chronological order of their original publication. I am grateful to Susan Beegel for her erudition and judgment in helping me to edit this volume.

My introduction begins by seeking Hemingway's place in American literary tradition and then relates *A Farewell to Arms* to the aesthetic impressionism of Walter Pater and Joseph Conrad. Daniel J. Schneider begins the chronological sequence with a study of the poetic imagery or "imagism" of *A Farewell to Arms*.

An investigation of tragic structure in the novel by Robert Merrill is followed by William Adair's Freudian account of *A Farewell to Arms* as Hemingway's own interpretation of the dreams, fantasies, and compulsions resulting from his early involvement in war.

Michael S. Reynolds compares Stephen Crane's *The Red Badge of Courage* to *Farewell,* and suggests that Hemingway, like Crane, relied upon imagination and not upon the autobiographical experience of battle. The palpable hostility of Hemingway toward women as the image of desire is traced in *Farewell* by Judith Fetterley, who confirms the earlier analysis by Leslie Fiedler which is cited in my introduction.

In a textual study of the novel's much rewritten conclusion, Bernard Oldsey attempts to illuminate Hemingway's choices among his multiple possibilities. Scott Donaldson skeptically reads the passivity and "innocence" of Frederic Henry as masking a wily self that calls the narrator's stance into question.

In Millicent Bell's interpretation, *A Farewell to Arms* is a coded system of feeling and judgment based upon Hemingway's war experiences on the Italian front. In a previously unpublished essay concluding this volume, Sandra Whipple Spanier sees Catherine Barkley as the true exemplar of Hemingway's code of heroism, since she manifests courage, loyalty, grace in confronting death, and a true ability to teach Frederic Henry what he badly needs to know. Spanier's argument is both feminist and shrewdly kind to Hemingway; it provokes skepticism in me, but itself shares in some of the qualities that Hemingway urged upon us.

Introduction

Hemingway freely proclaimed his relationship to *Huckleberry Finn*, and there is some basis for the assertion, except that there is little in common between the rhetorical stances of Twain and Hemingway. Kipling's *Kim*, in style and mode, is far closer to *Huckleberry Finn* than anything Hemingway wrote. The true accent of Hemingway's admirable style is to be found in an even greater and more surprising precursor:

> This grass is very dark to be from the white heads of old
>   mothers,
> Darker than the colorless beards of old men,
> Dark to come from under the faint red roofs of mouths.

Or again:

> I clutch the rails of the fence, my gore drips, thinn'd with the
>   ooze of my skin,
> I fall on the weeds and stones,
> The riders spur their unwilling horses, haul close,
> Taunt my dizzy ears and beat me violently over the head with
>   whip-stocks.
> Agonies are one of my changes of garments,
> I do not ask the wounded person how he feels, I myself become
>   the wounded person,
> My hurts turn livid upon me as I lean on a cane and observe.

Hemingway is scarcely unique in not acknowledging the paternity of Walt Whitman; T. S. Eliot and Wallace Stevens are far closer to Whitman than William Carlos Williams and Hart Crane were, but literary influence is a paradoxical and antithetical process, about which we continue to know all too little. The profound affinities between Hemingway,

1

Eliot, and Stevens are not accidental, but are family resemblances due to the repressed but crucial relation each had to Whitman's work. Hemingway characteristically boasted (in a letter to Sara Murphy, February 27, 1936) that he had knocked Stevens down quite handily: ". . . for statistics sake Mr. Stevens is 6 feet 2 weighs 225 lbs. and . . . when he hits the ground it is highly spectaculous." Since this match between the two writers took place in Key West on February 19, 1936, I am moved, as a loyal Stevensian, for statistics' sake to point out that the victorious Hemingway was born in 1899, and the defeated Stevens in 1879, so that the novelist was then going on thirty-seven, and the poet verging on fifty-seven. The two men doubtless despised one another, but in the letter celebrating his victory Hemingway calls Stevens "a damned fine poet" and Stevens always affirmed that Hemingway was essentially a poet, a judgment concurred in by Robert Penn Warren when he wrote that Hemingway "is essentially a lyric rather than a dramatic writer." Warren compared Hemingway to Wordsworth, which is feasible, but the resemblance to Whitman is far closer. Wordsworth would not have written, "I am the man, I suffer'd, I was there," but Hemingway almost persuades us he would have achieved that line had not Whitman set it down first.

II

It is now more than twenty years since Hemingway's suicide, and some aspects of his permanent canonical status seem beyond doubt. Only a few modern American novels seem certain to endure: *The Sun Also Rises, The Great Gatsby, Miss Lonelyhearts, The Crying of Lot 49,* and at least several by Faulkner, including *As I Lay Dying, Sanctuary, Light in August, The Sound and the Fury, Absalom, Absalom!* Two dozen stories by Hemingway could be added to the group, indeed perhaps all of *The First Forty-Nine Stories.* Faulkner is an eminence apart, but critics agree that Hemingway and Fitzgerald are his nearest rivals, largely on the strength of their shorter fiction. What seems unique is that Hemingway is the only American writer of prose fiction in this century who, as a stylist, rivals the principal poets: Stevens, Eliot, Frost, Hart Crane, aspects of Pound, W. C. Williams, Robert Penn Warren, and Elizabeth Bishop. This is hardly to say that Hemingway, at his best, fails at narrative or the representation of character. Rather, his peculiar excellence is closer to Whitman than to Twain, closer to Stevens than to Faulkner, and even closer to Eliot than to Fitzgerald, who was his friend and rival. He is an elegiac poet who mourns the self, who celebrates the self (rather less effectively) and who suffers divisions in the self. In the broadest tradition of American literature, he stems ultimately from the Emersonian reliance on the god within, which is the line of Whitman, Thoreau, and Dickinson. He arrives late and dark in this tradition, and is one of its negative theologians, as it were, but as in Stevens the negations, the cancellings, are never final. Even the most ferocious of his stories, say "God Rest You Merry, Gentlemen" or "A Natural History of the Dead," can be said to celebrate what we might call the Real Absence. Doc Fischer, in "God Rest You Merry, Gentlemen," is a precursor of Nathanael West's Shrike in *Miss Lonelyhearts,* and his savage, implicit religiosity prophesies not only Shrike's Satanic stance but the entire demonic world of Pynchon's explicitly paranoid or Luddite visions. Perhaps there was a nostalgia for a Catholic order always abiding in Hemingway's consciousness, but the cosmos of his fiction, early and late, is American Gnostic, as it was in Melville, who first developed so strongly the negative side of the Emersonian religion of self-reliance.

III

Hemingway notoriously and splendidly was given to overtly agonistic images whenever he described his relationship to canonical writers, including Melville, a habit of description in which he has been followed by his true ephebe, Norman Mailer. In a grand letter (September 6–7, 1949) to his publisher, Charles Scribner, he charmingly confessed, "Am a man without any ambition, except to be champion of the world, I wouldn't fight Dr. Tolstoi in a 20 round bout because I know he would knock my ears off." This modesty passed quickly, to be followed by, "If I can live to 60 I can beat him. (MAYBE)." Since the rest of the letter counts Turgenev, de Maupassant, Henry James, even Cervantes, as well as Melville and Dostoyevski, among the defeated, we can join Hemingway, himself, in admiring his extraordinary self-confidence. How justified was it, in terms of his ambitions?

It could be argued persuasively that Hemingway is the best short-story writer in the English language from Joyce's *Dubliners* until the present. The aesthetic dignity of the short story need not be questioned, and yet we seem to ask more of a canonical writer. Hemingway wrote *The Sun Also Rises* and not *Ulysses,* which is only to say that his true genius was for very short stories, and hardly at all for extended narrative. Had he been primarily a poet, his lyrical gifts would have sufficed: we do not hold it against Yeats that his poems, not his plays, are his principal glory. Alas, neither Turgenev nor Henry James, neither Melville nor Mark Twain provide true agonists for Hemingway. Instead, de Maupassant is the apter rival. Of Hemingway's intensity of style in the briefer compass, there is no question, but even *The Sun Also Rises* reads now as a series of epiphanies, of brilliant and memorable vignettes.

Much that has been harshly criticized in Hemingway, particularly in *For Whom the Bell Tolls,* results from his difficulty in adjusting his gifts to the demands of the novel. Robert Penn Warren suggests that Hemingway is successful when his "system of ironies and understatements is coherent." When incoherent, then, Hemingway's rhetoric fails as persuasion, which is to say, we read *To Have and Have Not* or *For Whom the Bell Tolls* and we are all too aware that the system of tropes is primarily what we are offered. Warren believes this not to be true of *A Farewell to Arms,* yet even the celebrated close of the novel seems now a worn understatement:

> But after I had got them out and shut the door and turned off the light it wasn't any good. It was like saying good-by to a statue. After a while I went out and left the hospital and walked back to the hotel in the rain.

Contrast this to the close of "Old Man at the Bridge," a story only two and a half pages long:

> There was nothing to do about him. It was Easter Sunday and the Fascists were advancing toward the Ebro. It was a gray overcast day with a low ceiling so their planes were not up. That and the fact that cats know how to look after themselves was all the good luck that old man would ever have.

The understatement continues to persuade here because the stoicism remains coherent, and is admirably fitted by the rhetoric. A very short story concludes itself by permanently troping the mood of a particular moment in history. Vignette is Hemingway's natural mode, or call it hard-edged vignette: a literary sketch that somehow seems to be the beginning or end of something longer, yet truly is complete in itself. Hemingway's style encloses what ought to be unenclosed, so that the genre remains subtle yet trades its charm for punch. But a novel of three hundred and forty pages (*A Farewell to Arms*) which I have just finished reading again (after twenty years away from it) cannot sustain itself upon the rhetoric of vignette. After many understatements, too many, the reader begins to believe that he is reading a Hemingway imitator, like the accomplished John O'Hara, rather than the master himself. Hemingway's notorious fault is the monotony of repetition, which becomes a dulling litany in a somewhat less accomplished imitator like Nelson Algren, and sometimes seems self-parody when we must confront it in Hemingway.

Nothing is got for nothing, and a great style generates defenses in us, particularly when it sets the style of an age, as the Byronic Hemingway did. As with Byron, the color and variety of the artist's life becomes something of a veil between the work and our aesthetic apprehension of it. Hemingway's career included four marriages (and three divorces); service as an ambulance driver for the Italians in World War I (with an honorable wound); activity as a war correspondent in the Greek-Turkish War (1922), the Spanish Civil War (1937–39), the Chinese-Japanese War (1941) and the War against Hitler in Europe (1944–45). Add big-game hunting and fishing, safaris, expatriation in France and Cuba, bullfighting, the Nobel prize, and ultimate suicide in Idaho, and you have an absurdly implausible life, apparently lived in imitation of Hemingway's own fiction. The final effect of the work and the life together is not less than mythological, as it was with Byron and with Whitman and with Oscar Wilde. Hemingway now is myth, and so is permanent as an image of American heroism, or perhaps more ruefully the American illusion of heroism. The best of Hemingway's work, the stories and *The Sun Also Rises*, are also a permanent part of the American mythology. Faulkner, Stevens, Frost, perhaps Eliot, and Hart Crane were stronger writers than Hemingway, but he alone in this American century has achieved the enduring status of myth.

IV

If *A Farewell to Arms* fails to sustain itself as a unified novel, it does remain Hemingway's strongest work after the frequent best of the short stories and *The Sun Also Rises*. It also participates in the aura of Hemingway's mode of myth, embodying as it does not only Hemingway's own romance with Europe but the permanent vestiges of our national romance with the Old World. The death of Catherine represents not the end of that affair, but its perpetual recurrence. I assign classic status in the interpretation of that death to Leslie Fiedler, with his precise knowledge of the limits of literary myth: "Only the dead woman becomes neither a bore nor a mother; and before Catherine can quite become either she must die, killed not by Hemingway, of course, but by childbirth!"

Fiedler finds a touch of Poe in this, but Hemingway seems to me far healthier. Death, to Poe, is after all less a metaphor for sexual fulfillment than it is an improvement over mere coition, since Poe longs for a union in essence and not just in act.

Any feminist critic who resents that too-lovely Hemingwayesque ending, in which Frederic Henry gets to walk away in the rain while poor Catherine takes the death for both of them, has my sympathy, if only because this sentimentality that mars the aesthetic effect is certainly the mask for a male resentment and fear of women. Hemingway's symbolic rain is read by Louis L. Martz as the inevitable trope for pity, and by Malcolm Cowley as a conscious symbol for disaster. A darker interpretation might associate it with Whitman's very American confounding of night, death, the mother, and the sea, a fourfold mingling that Whitman bequeathed to Wallace Stevens, T. S. Eliot, and Hart Crane, among many others. The death of the beloved woman in Hemingway is part of that tropological cosmos, in which the moist element dominates because death the mother is the true image of desire. For Hemingway, the rain replaces the sea, and is as much the image of longing as the sea is in Whitman or Hart Crane.

Robert Penn Warren, defending a higher estimate of *A Farewell to Arms* than I can achieve, interprets the death of Catherine as the discovery that "the attempt to find a substitute for universal meaning in the limited meaning of the personal relationship is doomed to failure." Such a reading, though distinguished, seems to me to belong more to the literary cosmos of T. S. Eliot than to that of Hemingway. Whatever nostalgia for transcendental verities Hemingway may have possessed, his best fiction invests its energies in the representation of personal relationships, and hardly with the tendentious design of exposing their inevitable inadequacies. If your personal religion quests for the matador as messiah, then you are likely to seek in personal relationships something of the same values enshrined in the ritual of bull and bullfighter: courage, dignity, the aesthetic exaltation of the moment, and an all but suicidal intensity of being—the sense of life gathered to a crowded perception and graciously open to the suddenness of extinction. That is a vivid but an unlikely scenario for an erotic association, at least for any that might endure beyond a few weeks.

Wyndham Lewis categorized Hemingway by citing Walter Pater on Prosper Merimée: "There is the formula . . . the enthusiastic amateur of rude, crude, naked force in men and women. . . . Painfully distinct in outline, inevitable to sight, unrelieved, there they stand." Around them,

Pater added, what Merimée gave you was "neither more nor less than empty space." I believe that Pater would have found more than that in Hemingway's formula, more in the men and women, and something other than empty space in their ambiance. Perhaps by way of Joseph Conrad's influence upon him, Hemingway had absorbed part at least of what is most meaningful in Pater's aesthetic impressionism. Hemingway's women and men know, with Pater, that we have an interval, and then our place knows us no more. Our one chance is to pack that interval with the multiplied fruit of consciousness, with the solipsistic truths of perception and sensation. What survives time's ravages in *A Farewell to Arms* is precisely Hemingway's textually embodied knowledge that art alone apprehends the moments of perception and sensation, and so bestows upon them their privileged status. Consider the opening paragraph of chapter 16:

> That night a bat flew into the room through the open door that led onto the balcony and through which we watched the night over the roofs of the town. It was dark in our room except for the small light of the night over the town and the bat was not frightened but hunted in the room as though he had been outside. We lay and watched him and I do not think he saw us because we lay so still. After he went out we saw a searchlight come on and watched the beam move across the sky and then go off and it was dark again. A breeze came in the night and we heard the men of the anti-aircraft gun on the next roof talking. It was cool and they were putting on their capes. I worried in the night about some one coming up but Catherine said they were all asleep. Once in the night we went to sleep and when I woke she was not there but I heard her coming along the hall and the door opened and she came back to the bed and said it was all right she had been downstairs and they were all asleep. She had been outside Miss Van Campen's door and heard her breathing in her sleep. She brought crackers and we ate them and drank some vermouth. We were very hungry but she said that would all have to be gotten out of me in the morning. I went to sleep again in the morning when it was light and when I was awake I found she was gone again. She came in looking fresh and lovely and sat on the bed and the sun rose while I had the thermometer in my mouth and we smelled the dew on the roofs and then the coffee of the men at the gun on the next roof.

The flight of the bat, the movement of the searchlight's beam and of the breeze, the overtones of the antiaircraft gunners blend into the light of the morning, to form a composite epiphany of what it is that Frederic Henry has lost when he finally walks back to the hotel in the rain. Can we define that loss? As befits the aesthetic impressionism of Pater, Conrad, Stephen Crane, and Hemingway, it is in the first place a loss of vividness and intensity in the world as experienced by the senses. In the aura of his love for Catherine, Frederic Henry knows the fullness of "It was dark" and "It was cool," and the smell of the dew on the roofs, and the aroma of the coffee being enjoyed by the anti-aircraft gunners. We are reminded that Pater's crucial literary ancestors were the unacknowledged Ruskin and the hedonistic visionary Keats, the Keats of the "Ode on Melancholy." Hemingway too, particularly in *A Farewell to Arms,* is an heir of Keats, with the poet's passion for sensuous immediacy, in all of its ultimate implications. Is not Catherine Barkley a belated and beautiful version of the goddess Melancholy, incarnating Keats's "Beauty that must die"? Hemingway too exalts that quester after the Melancholy,

> whose strenuous tongue
> Can burst Joy's grape against his palate fine;
> His soul shall taste the sadness of her might,
> And be among her cloudy trophies hung.

The Novel as Pure Poetry

Daniel J. Schneider

In a well-known essay Robert Penn Warren has drawn a distinction between two kinds of poetry, a "pure" poetry, which seeks more or less
systematically to exclude so-called "unpoetic" elements from its hushed
and hypnotic atmosphere, and an "impure," a poetry of inclusion or
synthesis, which welcomes into itself such supposedly recalcitrant and
inhospitable stuff as wit, cacophony, jagged rhythms, and intellectual
debate. The distinction between the two types, so helpful in the analysis
of lyrics, may obviously be employed to advantage in the criticism of
novels, and I should like to use it here to call attention to an aspect of
Hemingway's art that has not received any extended comment. For if
there are works, such as *War and Peace, Ulysses, Moby-Dick,* and *The Magic
Mountain,* whose power and beauty are best explained by their very "impurity"—novels that batten on the diversity of life and are most themselves when they are most "loose and baggy" (to use James's fine
phrase)—the strength of Hemingway's novels is explained best, I think,
by noting that they are in spirit and in method closer to pure lyric than
to epic, and that they systematically exclude whatever threatens to interfere with the illusion of life beheld under the aspect of a single, dominant,
all-pervasive mood or state of mind. They attempt to sustain perfectly a
single emotion: they begin with it and end with it, and any scenes,
characters, thoughts, or stylistic elements that might tend to weaken the
dominant emotion are ruthlessly rejected. Consequently, Hemingway's

From *Modern Fiction Studies* 14, no. 3 (Autumn 1968). © 1968 by the Purdue Research
Foundation, West Lafayette, Indiana.

art has both the virtues and the limitations of lyricism: maximum intensity on the one hand, extremely limited range on the other.

Hemingway's *A Farewell to Arms* is I think one of the purest lyric novels ever written. But if we are fully to appreciate its power—and the power of a number of other works by Hemingway—we are driven to examine the poetics of this lyricism and to assess, if we can, the extent to which Hemingway has exploited the possibilities of the type.

I

The dominant emotion or state of mind behind the events of *A Farewell to Arms* is seldom stated explicitly. It is always there, informing every scene of the novel, lying beneath every descriptive passage and every bit of characterization, but it seldom shows, or it shows, at most, but a tiny part of itself, like the iceberg that Hemingway often took to be the apt image of his art. It is a bitterness, a disgust, a desolation of soul, a remorse of such depth and durance that it can be held in check only by dint of the severest, most unremitting self-control. When it does show itself clearly, this inner violence, as in chapter 34 of *Farewell,* it is expressed in this way:

> If people bring so much courage to this world the world has to kill them to break them, so of course it kills them. The world breaks every one and afterward many are strong at the broken places. But those that will not break it kills. It kills the very good and the very gentle and the very brave impartially. If you are none of these you can be sure it will kill you too but there will be no special hurry.

The world's malevolence is taken for granted in Hemingway's novels. The artistic problem Hemingway faced was to find the correlatives of his bitterness—objects adequate to the emotion, techniques capable of rendering it as purely as possible. The tragic action, involving failure, humiliation, and, especially, the punishment and defeat of lovers was of course the chief means of conveying the essential vision, the essential bitterness. But a whole poetics of the novel which confines itself to the embodiment of such a state of mind had to be developed, and it is in the solution of minor as well as of major problems that the genius of Hemingway is finally revealed. His style, for example—the perfect correlative (as Brooks and Warren have shown) of his sense of the ruthless and arbitrary condition of the world that breaks and kills—becomes the perfect correlative too of the emotions of despair and bitterness. The careful selection of a dominant image and its reiteration through whole paragraphs and pages and chapters, so that the image presently becomes symbol, conveying both the central meaning and the central emotion, becomes Hemingway's fixed method. Perhaps the best analogy is found in the choice of a musical key and in the elaborate harmonization of notes always referring to the tonic. Ideally, when the writing is purest, every sentence will bespeak the central meaning and emotion. There will be no purely functional passages, no passages which merely illustrate a meaning, no characters or episodes given freedom to develop emotions outside the dominant bitterness. Everything will be converted into a symbol of the emotion. Where such conversion does not take place, the art fails and the novel becomes epic, not lyric; narrative, instead of the pure utterance of passion.

The determination to make the novel lyrical inevitably influences all of its parts. Character becomes, in one sense, unimportant. Characters exist for the sake of the emotion and, as in most lyric poems, need not be three-dimensional. Indeed, any full and vivid particularization of character is likely to work against the dominant emotion, for when a character is complex and fully realized, he is scarcely able to maintain a single, fixed emotion or state of mind. It is only rather highly generalized characters who can feel "purely." A lovely and brave young woman may function well in a lyric world. Represent her in such complicated terms as Joyce employs to depict Leopold Bloom and the emotion is adulterated by a thousand reservations and ironic complexities. Of course character cannot be *reduced* to passion: a writer like Poe frequently fails because he is so much interested in feeling that he virtually eliminates character altogether; but Poe's Gothic tales suggest the proper direction of the lyric novel: character must exist for the sake of the emotion, and wherever the variety and diversity of life threaten to dilute or dissipate the central emotion, life must be excluded from the novel. It is thus no fair criticism to say that Hemingway has created no memorable characters; the truth is that his novels necessarily reject such people. One may imagine what Hemingway would have to do with the "memorable" Buck Mulligan to adjust him to the world of *Farewell*. Much of the élan of the Joycean character would necessarily be sacrificed to the mood of the scene, and only so much of Mulligan's irreverence as would not undermine the sense of despair would be recorded. In short, what is rollicking insouciance in Joyce would become, in Hemingway, the doleful chant of "irony and pity"; the Rabelaisian humor would be infused with the central bitterness, and would scarcely be humor at all: Mulligan would become Rinaldi.

The action, too, must obviously become, as nearly as possible, simple, intellectually uncomplicated, and, in spirit if not in actual construction, akin to lyric soliloquy. An action involving much intellectual debate, analysis, repartee, or a multiplication of points of view is clearly antithetical to the spirit of Hemingway's lyric novels. For cerebration tends to destroy passion; intellectual analysis or agility introduces a note of objectivity that the lyric novel cannot tolerate, and debate might require the introduction of spokesmen whose personalities and whose mere presence could shatter the lyric mood. It is for this reason that the action of Hemingway's lyric novels approaches, whenever it can, the scene of prolonged suffering. The characteristic sources of complication are not new complications of "plot" in the sense that fresh *problems* are introduced to be debated and solved, but rather new wounds, new torments, so that bitterness deepens and grows toward a pitch of anguish and remorse. Hemingway is always reluctant to introduce actions that do not feed the dominant emotion (sometimes so close to self-pity) and in consequence his characteristic way of structuring the action of his novels is to employ a simple qualitative shift or oscillation between despair and happiness. In *The Sun Also Rises* the shifts are from Paris, to Burguete, to Pamplona, to San Sebastian; in *A Farewell to Arms* they are from the front, to the hospital, to the front, to Switzerland: disgust and bitterness, followed by a short respite, then back to disgust and bitterness again. The dominant emotion is intensified through these powerful contrasts with opposite emotions. And major form is reinforced by minor: brief scenes in which characters are represented as enjoying intensely food and drink or a lovely view or a simple physical comfort exist chiefly to heighten the sense of despair and bitterness; the interludes of normal pleasure are inevitably short-lived; by various signs we know that they will soon be over and that whatever one has will be taken away. Every meal, every sight, every sound thus comes to one as to a man about to be executed. That is one reason the descriptions of food and drink always seem so preternaturally vivid in Hemingway.

It is unnecessary to extend this poetics further at this point. We shall see, if we look closely at *A Farewell to Arms,* how thoroughly Hemingway has exploited the possibilities of his lyric form.

II

In *A Farewell to Arms* the dominant state of mind—the sense of death, defeat, failure, nothingness, emptiness—is conveyed chiefly by the image of the rain (with all its tonal associates, *mist, wet, damp, river, fog*), by images and epithets of desolation (chiefly *bare, thin, small,* and *fallen leaves*), and by images and epithets of impurity and corruption (chiefly *dust, mud, dirt,* and *disease*). Hemingway's method of working with the images is surprisingly uniform. I have already employed an analogy to music; another way of describing the method is to think of a painter working tiny patches of a dominant color over his entire canvas. Hemingway himself perhaps had both analogies in mind when he said, in the Lillian Ross interview, that he had "learned how to make a landscape from Mr. Paul Cézanne" and mentioned, in the same context, his imitation of Bach's counterpoint in the first chapter of *Farewell*. The images are repeated so frequently that they begin to toll like bells in the mind. Virtually every sentence says, "Death, despair, failure, emptiness," because virtually every sentence contains an image or symbol associated with the dominant state of mind.

The novel begins with this state of mind, and it is established so firmly, through the repetition of the central symbols, that any emotions other than bitterness and despair may thereafter intrude only with difficulty. The typical procedure, as in lyric poetry, is to intensify the dominant emotion by means of a simple contrast of images. Thus the images of purity and vitality, introduced in the second sentence of the novel, are contrasted throughout the chapter with the images of dirt and failure:

> In the late summer of that year we lived in a house in a village that looked across the river and the plain to the mountains. In the bed of the river there were pebbles and boulders, dry and white in the sun, and the water was clear and swiftly moving and blue in the channels. Troops went by the house and down the road and the dust they raised powdered the leaves of the trees. The trunks of the trees too were dusty and the leaves fell early that year and we saw the troops marching along the road and the dust rising and leaves, stirred by the breeze, falling and the soldiers marching and afterward the road bare and white except for the leaves.

Purity has been defiled, the life-force has been thwarted and defeated. The leaves are "powdered" by dust; the trunks too are "dusty"; the leaves fall "early"; and the empty road, "bare and white except for the leaves," becomes a perfect correlative of the inner desolation. The defilement and violation of life is further suggested by a reference to camouflage ("There were big guns that passed in the day drawn by tractors, the long barrels of the guns covered with green branches and green leafy branches and vines laid over the tractor") and by a reference to the cartridge-boxes bulging under the capes of the soldiers "so that the men, passing on the road, marched as though they were six months gone with child." And these bitter ironies are reinforced by the introduction of the dominant symbol of the rain: not life-giving rain causing the leaves to grow but the autumnal and winter rain causing them to fall, a rain associated with darkness, mud, and death:

> There was fighting for that mountain too, but it was not suc-
> cessful, and in the fall when the rains came the leaves all fell
> from the chestnut trees and the branches were bare and the
> trunks were black with rain. The vineyards were thin and
> bare-branched too and all the country wet and brown and dead
> with the autumn. There were mists over the river and clouds
> on the mountain and the trucks splashed mud on the road and
> the troops were muddy and wet in their capes; their rifles were
> wet.

The sense of failure and impotence is also reinforced by the studious avoidance of action verbs. Almost invariably Hemingway employs the copulative *to be,* and the expletives *there were* and *there was* occur ten times in the twenty-one sentences of the chapter, six of the sentences being introduced by them. The repetitions give a sense of endless sameness and weariness: abandon hope, all ye who enter here.

The concluding paragraphs of the chapter reinforce what has already been established powerfully. The guns, the tractors, the motor-cars show a ruthless power, and it is as if life, in the presence of these overwhelming forces of death, had withered and shrunk. The "very small" king, sitting in the speeding motor-car "between two generals," becomes a fine correlative of the sense of impotence:

> There were small gray motor cars that passed going very fast;
> usually there was an officer in the seat with the driver and
> more officers in the back seat. They splashed more mud than
> the camions even and if one of the officers in the back was
> very small and sitting between two generals, he himself so
> small that you could not see his face but only the top of his
> cap and his narrow back, and if the car went especially fast it
> was probably the king. He lived in Udine and came out in this
> way nearly every day to see how things were going, and things
> went very badly.

> At the start of the winter came the permanent rain and with
> the rain came the cholera. But it was checked and in the end
> only seven thousand died of it in the army.

With this last paragraph the sense of doom is complete. The rain is "permanent" and the apparent consolation, the fact that the cholera is checked, is viciously undercut by the irony that "*only* seven thousand died of it in the army."

The mood of the first chapter is thus established powerfully through the proliferation of associated images, images written in a single key. But to continue in this way—that is, to continue to present events and people as the objectification of feeling through the modulation of images—would of course be to drive narrative out of the novel; there would be no "story," only bitterness distilled. Hemingway's artistic problem accordingly becomes that of presenting action and conflict in such a way that the central emotion will not be shattered by the inclusion of elements hostile to it. As I have indicated, action must be converted into passion; characters must become embodiments of the central bitterness. When it becomes necessary, then, in chapter 2, to introduce characters and to develop a scene whose essential quality is potentially uncongenial to the established emotion, Hemingway must take pains to weaken or nullify the inharmonious effects and to absorb character and scene into the dominant mood. So it is that when the priest, the captain, and the other soldiers are introduced, Hemingway guards against any dilution of the central emotion by framing the scene with a description expressive, once again, of the profound regret and bitterness:

> Later, below in the town, I watched the snow falling, looking
> out of the window of the bawdy house, the house for officers,
> where I sat with a friend and two glasses drinking a bottle of
> Asti, and, looking out at the snow falling slowly and heavily,
> we knew it was all over for that year. Up the river the moun-
> tains had not been taken; none of the mountains beyond the
> river had been taken. That was all left for next year. My friend
> saw the priest from our mess going by in the street, walking
> carefully in the slush, and pounded on the window to attract
> his attention. The priest looked up. He saw us and smiled. My
> friend motioned for him to come in. The priest shook his head
> and went on. That night in the mess after the spaghetti course
> . . . the captain commenced picking on the priest.

In the scene that follows, the captain's baiting of the priest takes its tone from the frame and is anything but humorous. The "good fun" is swallowed up by the pervasive sadness and bitterness, and the episode acts upon the reader in much the same way as an episode in *The Waste Land* affects Eliot's readers: dialogue, narrative, description are all viewed as expressions of the central fears and desires. The characters introduced are not important in themselves; their development as characters does not interest the writer. They are aspects of the hero's state of mind, and represent, covertly, the conflicts of his soul.

We must note, moreover, that the scene is, characteristically, short. For to lengthen any scene of this sort, in which the actions and speeches of minor characters threaten to shake our awareness of the hero's mood, would be fatal to the lyric novel. If developed at length, the scene would cease to function as the token of the hero's feelings. E. M. Forster, in his *Aspects of the Novel,* has pointed out the danger of the characters' taking the story out of the novelist's control. The minor characters, if freed from the hero's sensibility, would take the scene into their own hands. The rhythm and mood of the scene would be theirs, not the hero's, and the scene, instead of reinforcing, might easily weaken or dissipate the central emotion. Furthermore, any particularly vivid rendering of the inherent "coloring" of the events and speeches—such rendering as one finds everywhere in the novels of Dickens—might work dangerously against the emotion. Hence the scene must be reported as barely, as "objectively" as possible. Perhaps it has not been sufficiently appreciated that "objectivity," as employed by Hemingway, is more than a means of effective understatement or of being true to the facts; it is also, much of the time, a means of preventing alien attitudes and feelings from asserting themselves vigorously—at the expense of the dominant emotion of the lyric novel. Of course objectivity *also* gives an air of distance and detachment; but where the objectively rendered scene is framed by lyric passages of great intensity, the scene becomes suffused with the emotion of the antecedent lyric, and it is precisely the deadpan reporting with the recurrent "he saids" that *permits* such penetration of the emotion.

The depression of Frederic Henry continues into chapter 3, but by this time the impressions of bitterness and failure have accumulated so densely that one is ready for a shift to an opposite state of mind. Returning from his leave, Frederic finds everything at the front unchanged. He has not gone to Abruzzi, as the priest urged him to, and, as the symbolism suggests delicately, he is mired in moral filth and inertia. Rinaldi, after kissing him, says, "You're dirty. . . . You ought to wash," and in chapter 4 Frederic observes, "I was very dusty and dirty and went up to my room to wash." In truth he needs a kind of purification. Thus when he sees Catherine Barkley for the first time in the garden of the British hospital, the imagery hints at the purity, the Edenlike peace that Frederic most deeply craves: "Miss Barkley was in the garden. Another nurse was with her. We saw their white uniforms through the trees and walked toward them." But the first conversation of the lovers, with its truncated, tight-lipped exchanges, only reiterates the desperation and despair that have already pervaded the novel. Once a key word has been sounded, Hemingway modulates it beautifully in half a dozen different shadings, until the conversation, like the descriptions already quoted, becomes a refrain on the theme of failure:

> "Yes," she said. "People can't realize what France is like. If they did, it couldn't go on. He didn't have a sabre cut. They blew him all to bits."
>
> I didn't say anything.
>
> "Do you suppose it will always go on?"
>
> "No."
>
> "What's to stop it?"
>
> "It will crack somewhere."
>
> "We'll crack. We'll crack in France. They can't go on doing things like the Somme and not crack."
>
> "They won't crack here," I said.
>
> "You think not?"
>
> "No. They did very well last summer."
>
> "They may crack," she said. "Anybody may crack."
>
> "The Germans too."
>
> "No," she said. "I think not."

Catherine here exists almost as the echo of Frederic's own bitterness and despair. She is Despair turning desperately to the religion of love. She has no past beyond the absolute minimum required for plausibility. Like another Catherine, Brontë's Catherine Earnshaw, she *is* her lover: her temperamental affinity to Frederic is so marked that their right to each other is accepted almost from the first moment of meeting. Thus she is, in a sense, not a distinct character at all but Frederic's bitterness or his desire objectified. She will presently become the peace or bliss that stands at farthest remove from the war: the white snows of the mountaintops, the idyllic serenity of Switzerland, the Beatrice of the *Paradiso*.

To lose her will be to lose Love. The lyric novel requires no deeper characterization.

Once she has been introduced, Hemingway is ready to effect the first qualitative shift in the novel. He has only to bring about the circumstances that will make possible a brief interlude of love and joy—a state of mind opposite to the intolerable mood of the opening chapters. In chapter 7 Frederic returns to the front, and the sweat, the heat, and the dust are again emphasized. References to washing or taking baths recur, and in chapter 9, when he is wounded, we are told that so much dirt has blown into the wound that it has not hemorrhaged much. The form of the next several chapters, then, becomes the gradual emergence from the filth and darkness of the war into the purity and light of love. The slow healing of Frederic's wound is concomitant with a subtle, incomplete healing of his soul, and before his return to the front he will have acquired, though without fully knowing it, the conviction that neither Rinaldi, who visits him in chapter 10, nor the priest, who visits him in chapter 11, can claim his soul: his love of Catherine is his religion. Yet this first idyll of love is by no means as pure and satisfying as the second interlude in Switzerland. It alters Frederic's disposition; it teaches him that love is possible; but it does not bring such full and radiant joy as will come later. It must, of necessity, be less complete, less satisfying, than the Switzerland episodes; if it were not, the happiness in Switzerland would be anticlimactic, and there would be no conviction that the lovers had grown emotionally and spiritually in such a way as to make the shattering of their union fully tragic. At this stage of the action Hemingway therefore wisely presents only so much of the lovers' joy as will establish a strong contrast between the old state of mind and the new. The moments of joy are intermittent. There are still, even after Frederic's recovery, many ominous suggestions of the old hollowness and despair. The ugliness of Etore's ambition to rise and win glory in the army reminds the lovers of the world they want to forget. The rain returns and Catherine, who sometimes sees herself "dead in it," is frightened and begins to cry; in chapter 20 the dishonesty of the fixed horse-races sullies the lovers' afternoon, though they are able to outwit the world by betting on a horse they've never heard of (named symbolically "Light for Me") and Catherine says, "I feel so much cleaner." But in chapter 21 Catherine announces that she is pregnant, and the uncertainty of the future stirs a new dread. In the next chapter the rain returns: "It turned cold that night and the next day it was raining. Coming home from the Ospedale Maggiore it rained very hard and I was wet when I came in.

Up in my room the rain was coming down heavily outside on the balcony, and the wind blew it against the glass doors." Frederic comes down with jaundice, a physical correlative of the old sense of "rottenness," and the visit he and Catherine had planned to Pallanza is now out of the question. The old pattern of failure reasserts itself. When Miss Van Campen discovers the empty bottles in the armoire of his hospital room, his leave is cancelled.

In chapter 23, the night on which Frederic returns to the front, the rain, the lovers' goodbyes, and the sense of helplessness all combine to produce a profound pathos and anguish that passes, finally, into a bitterness even more intense than that of the opening chapters. The chapter begins with Frederic's making arrangements to have a seat on the troop train held for him and with his saying goodbye at the hospital. The wife of the porter weeps. Frederic walks to a wineshop and waits for Catherine to pass. At this point the rain of despair and death is suggested only by mist and fog: "It was dark outside and cold and misty. . . . There was a fog in the square and when we came close to the front of the cathedral it was very big and the stone was wet." Frederic asks Catherine if she would like to go in, but she says no, and they go instead to a hotel where the furniture of vice, red plush curtains, a satin coverlet on the bed, and "many mirrors," besmirch the sacredness of their love. On their trip to the hotel the fog changes to rain, and the sense of failure and loss deepens:

> "We can get a cab at the bridge," I said. We stood on the bridge *in the fog* waiting for a carriage. Several streetcars passed, full of people going home. Then a carriage came along but there was someone in it. *The fog was turning to rain.*
> "We could walk or take a tram," Catherine said.
> "One will be along," I said. "They go by here."
> "Here one comes," she said.
> The driver stopped his horse and lowered the metal sign on his meter. The top of the carriage was up and there were *drops of water* on the driver's coat. His varnished hat was *shining in the wet*. We sat back in the seat together and the top of the carriage made it dark. [Italics mine.]

In the hotel Catherine bursts out, "I never felt like a whore before." Frederic stands at the window looking down at "the wet pavement" until Catherine calls him back to bed. For a time the lovers are happy in the hotel room, which, in a bitter irony, Catherine refers to as their "fine house" and their "home." But in a moment of stillness they can "hear the rain" and presently they must leave. The symbolic rain now finds its way into almost every sentence, as if doom were complete, inescapable:

> I saw the carriage coming. It stopped, the horse's head hanging *in the rain,* and the waiter stepped out, *opened his umbrella,* and came toward the hotel. We met him at the door and walked out *under the umbrella* down *the wet walk* to the carriage at the curb. *Water was running in the gutter.*
>
> "There is your package on the seat," the waiter said. He stood *with the umbrella* until we were in and I had tipped him.
>
> "Many thanks. Pleasant journey," he said. The coachman lifted the reins and the horse started. The waiter turned away *under the umbrella* and went toward the hotel. We drove down the street and turned to the left, then came around to the right in front of the station. There were two carabinieri standing under the light just *out of the rain.* The light shone on their hats. *The rain* was clear and transparent against the light from the station. A porter came out from under the shelter of the station, his shoulders up *against the rain.* [Italics mine.]

When Frederic enters the crowded troop-train, where "every one was hostile," the return to the old bitterness is virtually complete. He gives up his seat to the belligerent captain with the "new and shiny" scar, then stands watching the lights of the station as the train pulls out. Light has been associated from the beginning with Catherine, her white uniform and, especially, her shining hair. Just before boarding the train, Frederic sees her face "in the light." But now "It was still raining and soon the windows were wet and you could not see out." The violence of the shift from the interlude of love to the nightmare of the war is consummately rendered in the final sentences of the chapter: Frederic is swallowed up in a hell of darkness, congestion, and hostility, and the loss of his identity as lover is complete; he sleeps on the floor of the corridor, thinking: "they could all walk over me if they wouldn't step on me. Men were sleeping on the floor all down the corridor. Others stood holding on to the window rods or leaning against the doors. That train was always crowded."

The world has again triumphed. Accordingly, the sense of desolation and failure at the beginning of book 3 is almost identical with that of the novel's first chapter. Once again it is autumn, and once again Hemingway uses the limited palette of key words to paint the emotion, building his opening paragraph on the adjective "bare" and on references to the rain and to "shrunken" life:

Now in the fall the trees were all *bare* and the roads were muddy. I rode to Gorizia from Udine on a camion. We passed other camions on the road and I looked at the country. The mulberry trees were *bare* and the fields were brown. There were *wet* dead leaves on the road from the rows of *bare* trees and men were working on the road, tamping stone in the ruts from piles of crushed stone along the side of the road between the trees. We saw the town *with a mist over it* that cut off the mountains. We crossed the river and I saw that it was running high. *It had been raining* in the mountains. We came into the town past the factories and then the houses and villas and I saw many more houses had been hit. On a narrow street we passed a British Red Cross ambulance. The driver wore a cap and his face was *thin* and very tanned. I did not know him. I got down from the camion in the big square in front of the Town Major's house, the driver handed down my rucksack and I put it on and swung on the two musettes and walked to our villa. It did not feel like a homecoming.

I walked down the *damp* gravel driveway looking at the villa through the trees. The windows were all shut but the door was open. I went in and found the major sitting at a table in the *bare* room with maps and typed sheets of paper on the wall. [Italics mine.]

The old sense of pollution also returns: Rinaldi, who fears he has syphilis, chides Frederic for trying to cleanse his conscience with a toothbrush. And the sense of impotence and failure is further objectified in Rinaldi's "You can't do it. You can't do it. I say you can't do it. You're dry and you're empty and there's nothing else. There's nothing else I tell you." Presently Frederic picks up the refrain: he believes "in sleep," he tells the priest, "meaning nothing." Then in chapter 27 the rains begin again:

It stormed all that day. The wind drove down *the rain* and everywhere there was *standing water* and mud. The plaster of the broken houses was gray and *wet.* Late in the afternoon the rain stopped and from out number two post I saw the *bare wet* autumn country with clouds over the tops of the hills and the straw screening over the roads *wet and dripping.* The sun came out once before it went down and shone on the *bare* woods beyond the ridge. . . . We loaded two cars and drove down

the road that was screened with *wet* mats and the last of the
sun came through in the breaks between the strips of matting.
Before we were out on the clear road behind the hill the sun
was down. We went on down the clear road and as it turned
into the open and went into the square arched tunnel of matting *the rain started again.*

The wind rose in the night and at three o'clock in the morning *with the rain coming in sheets* there was a bombardment and
the Croatians came over across the mountain meadows and
through the patches of wood and into the front line. They
fought *in the dark in the rain* and a counter-attack of scared
men from the second line drove them back. There was much
shelling and many rockets *in the rain* and machine-gun and
rifle fire all along the line. They did not come again and it was
quieter and between *the gusts of wind and rain* we could hear
the sound of a great bombardment far to the north. [Italics
mine.]

The retreat begins, "orderly, wet and sullen," with troops marching
"under the rain." In chapter 27 the word "rain" appears twenty-four
times; in chapter 28, seventeen times. Chapter 27 begins with a reference
to sleep—meaning, of course, nothing—and in twelve pages the word
appears, incredibly, as noun, adjective, or verb, thirty-three times. I am
aware that such counting is not in itself a proof of the lyric progression
of these events, but when rain means death and sleep means nothing, the
recurrence of the words builds a mood of absolute hopelessness.

Moreover, because of the repetitions, a note of desperation comes to
suffuse the scene: the pressure of the accumulated bitterness will become
too intense, and the dominant emotion will again seek to elicit its opposite, pure peace, pure happiness, the pure joy of love. After the overwhelming development of the emotion in these chapters, Frederic's bolt
for freedom cannot be far off. Hemingway can sustain the emotion for
a few chapters more, but any further prolongation would make the intensity commonplace and the evil banal, meaningless. Frederic must soon
fall into the hands of the battle-police. A very brief qualitative shift in
chapter 30 enables Hemingway to prolong the suffering for an additional
chapter: the interlude in the barn depicts a normality, a wholesomeness
and sanity that appear with great force after the nightmare of the retreat
("The hay smelled good and lying in the hay took away all the years in
between. We had lain in hay and talked and shot sparrows with an air-

rifle when they perched in the triangle cut high up in the wall of the barn"), but the war is too close, the barn provides only momentary respite, and Frederic must quickly move out into the "black night with the rain." The scene in which he confronts the battle-police occurs within four pages after the departure from the barn.

Once Frederic has fled, the lyric form of the novel is predictable: the interlude in Switzerland followed by the crushing failure in the hospital. Once again the rhythm of the novel becomes that of emergence from darkness and failure. The rain continues as Frederic crosses the symbolic Venetian plain (chap. 31), as he takes the train to Stresa, and as he and Catherine lie in the hotel room there (chap. 34). In chapter 35 there occurs a brief interlude of sanity and peace in which Frederic trolls for lake trout with the barman and plays billiards with Count Greffi; but chapter 36 begins, "That night there was a storm and I woke to hear the rain lashing the window-panes," and in "the dark and the rain" Frederic and Catherine set out for Switzerland. In chapter 37 Frederic rows all night as the rain comes "occasionally in gusts." But when they set foot in Switzerland a second and more perfect idyll of love and purity commences.

Here again, as in the earlier interlude, Hemingway wisely guards against sentimentalizing the period of happiness. The religion of love is not enough: there is anxiety about the future, and Catherine is quick to notice that Frederic is chafing because he has nothing to do. But after the prolonged suffering and failure of the middle section of the novel, the impression of perfect joy is very strong, and the emotion is objectified in dozens of images suggesting sanity, wholesomeness, purity, and peace. Energy returns: "it was good walking on the road and invigorating." The snow on the mountain peaks, like the snows of Kilimanjaro, is a correlative of the sense of heavenly bliss and purity. The sun shines, and the air is "cold and clear." By January the winter settles into "bright cold days and hard cold nights." The snow is now "clean packed"; the air comes "sharply into your lungs"; there is now a sense that the life-force has *not* been defeated, and the lovers see foxes; the night is "dry and cold and very clear."

It is not until March, when the winter breaks (chap. 40) and it begins raining that the old failure and bitterness threaten to shatter the lovers' happiness. Then, in the magnificent last chapter, the pattern of failure is sharply reasserted in a terrible echo of Rinaldi's "You can't do it." All of Catherine's efforts to give birth to the child fail. She cries out that the anesthetic is "not working." The child is strangled by the umbilical cord;

the caesarian fails. Even Frederic's effort to say good-by fails: "It wasn't any good. It was like saying good-by to a statue." And so he is delivered up, once again, to the rain of death and failure: "After a while I went out and left the hospital and walked back to the hotel in the rain." The two attempts to escape the world's malice have failed, just as, in *The Sun Also Rises,* the two interludes of sanity and purity (the trout-fishing episode and the swimming episode at San Sebastian) provide only brief respite from the world; and one is left with the conviction that any further effort to escape will be crushed with equal ruthlessness.

The basic rhythm of the action of *Farewell* is thus almost identical with that of Hemingway's earlier novel, and the symbolism, too, is virtually unchanged. It seems safe to say that Hemingway had established his art in the earlier book: he had learned that lyricism was his essential talent, and he set about deliberately to apply the knowledge imparted by the earlier lessons. Over the next thirty years he was not to make any significant changes in his basic method. If there was a slight decline in his creative energy in the later books, if some of them seem mechanical, their style having become self-conscious mannerism rather than the perfect objectification of lyric impulses, the defects were scarcely so great as to impair the central vitality of his work. For he had developed his lyric art with the utmost attention to every means of rendering emotion purely. By 1929 he knew so well what he could do and how he could do it that he had reduced the possibilities of failure to a minimum. To adventure into the epic novel might have proved disastrous to an artist of Hemingway's limited powers. Provided that he confined himself to the lyric art he knew so thoroughly, he was not likely to fail. It is perhaps no small part of his genius that he seems to have recognized his limitations and to have made maximum use of the materials available to his lyric sensibility.

Tragic Form in *A Farewell to Arms*

Robert Merrill

I doubt very much that we need a "new" reading of Hemingway's *A Farewell to Arms*. The novel has been discussed many times, often intelligently. No one would suggest that it is a "problem" in the sense that *Billy Budd* is a problem, or *The Turn of the Screw*. I do think, however, that a basic question about the book has been somewhat neglected. This is a matter of its form. *A Farewell to Arms* is probably Hemingway's most admired novel, but few critics have taken seriously his suggestion that the book is a tragedy. I think this is unfortunate, for it obscures Hemingway's contribution to the history of tragic form.

There is little question that Hemingway conceived of *A Farewell to Arms* as a tragedy. He once referred to the novel as his *Romeo and Juliet* and later wrote: "The fact that the book was a tragic one did not make me unhappy since I believed that life was a tragedy and knew it could only have one end." Why, then, have Hemingway's critics resisted this classification? Basically, they have asked how much we can feel toward such "victims" as Frederic Henry and Catherine Barkley, the novel's hero and heroine. They have argued that *A Farewell to Arms* is not a tragedy because its lovers make no fatal error in judgment or deed and suffer a "catastrophe" which is merely accidental. They have insisted that Hemingway's lovers are not responsible for what happens to them, whereas moral responsibility is at the heart of tragedy.

Hemingway's critics have obviously read their Aristotle. And they are right, of course, in suggesting that *A Farewell to Arms* is not Aristotle's idea of a tragedy. Since Aristotle it has been thought necessary to tragedy

From *American Literature* 45, no. 4 (January 1974). © 1974 by Duke University Press.

that the doom of the hero issue from his own acts. The hero may be flawed in knowledge or character—depending on one's reading of the *Poetics*—but his downfall must derive from this "flaw." Hemingway clearly departs from this traditional formula. Whereas the tragic catastrophe is supposed to result from the hero's mistaken actions, tragedy in *A Farewell to Arms* depends on Frederic Henry doing the one thing we most desire him to do and most respect him for doing—committing himself in love to Catherine Barkley. There is nothing inherently tragic about this, except in the world of *A Farewell to Arms*, where the tragic resolution depends on just this admirable decision. Hemingway has fashioned a new form of tragedy in which the hero acts not mistakenly but supremely well, and suffers a doom which is not directly caused by his actions at all. The belief that life is a tragedy, *life* itself, has become the backbone for a new literary structure.

But why call this structure tragic? Ultimately, the answer must be that it produces a tragic effect. I believe that is not only my experience but the experience of anyone who can identify with Hemingway's lovers. The crucial point is that in *A Farewell to Arms*, as in any tragic work, we are made to feel that the hero's doom is inevitable. If the reader doubts that Hemingway has achieved this sense of tragic inevitability, let him consider whether the book could have ended with the lovers' escape to Switzerland rather than Catherine's death. This is no more possible than that Macbeth should be forgiven his sins and restored to virtue, or Lear allowed to live out his days with the faithful Cordelia. It is not possible because Hemingway has created tragic expectations from the outset. These expectations condition our response to the book throughout. As in any tragedy, they must be satisfied if the work is to succeed.

I am suggesting that Hemingway has achieved a tragic effect without relying on the conventions of classical tragedy. If this is so, there are important implications for the theory of tragedy. But before glancing at these implications, we should explore the means by which Hemingway has produced this effect. Specifically, how does Hemingway create the tragic expectations I have referred to?

Our forebodings largely derive from the nature of Hemingway's fictional world. Because it is so important to his intended effect, Hemingway employs every possible device in rendering this world. At several points he has Frederic Henry comment on it directly: when he reflects on the remarks of Gino, the Italian patriot, in the famous passage which begins, "I was always embarrassed by the words sacred, glorious, and sacrifice and the expression in vain"; when he meditates on Catherine's courage: "If people bring so much courage to this world the world has to kill them to break them, so of course it kills them. . . . It kills the very good and the very gentle and the very brave impartially"; when he awaits Catherine's death: "You did not know what it was about. You never had time to learn. They threw you in and told you the rules and the first time they caught you off base they killed you." But even such commentary as this, coming from Hemingway's hero, is not the principal means by which a brutal, chaotic universe is introduced into the novel. The nature of this world is dramatized from the beginning. On the first page of the novel Frederic looks out upon an endless line of Italian troops, "pregnant" not with life but with "6.5 mm. cartridges." Life in this world is such that it can be said of the cholera, "in the end *only* seven thousand died of it in the army" (my emphasis). The devastation of the war is suggested in the second chapter, once Frederic moves with his unit to Gorizia. Here "the forest of oak trees on the mountain beyond the town was gone. The forest had been green in the summer when we had come into the town but now there were the stumps and the broken trunks and the ground torn up." This world where "only" seven thousand die of cholera, where trees have given way to stumps and broken trunks, where men carry death and not life—this world is not one in which "normal" moral standards are likely to stand unsullied. Thus we first meet our hero in a brothel. And the first recorded dialogue involves the baiting of the priest by Italian officers.

In these and other ways, Hemingway suggests at once the bad world his people must confront. Its obvious and overwhelming manifestation is the war itself. Frederic's experiences more than justify the bitterness he reveals in the passages quoted above. He is blown up while eating a piece of cheese, a dead soldier bleeds all over him as he is transported from the front, he is thrust back into the war only to participate in the nightmarish Caporetto retreat, and finally he is almost executed by his own army. And everyone about him suffers similarly. His favorite subordinates, Passini and Aymo, are killed "unreasonably"; Rinaldi, his best friend, ends in a depression which has only two comforts, and "one is bad for my work and the other is over in half an hour or fifteen minutes"; even the priest is finally "discouraged." The chaos without either kills or destroys the strength within. It is finally so bad that Frederic must make his famous "separate peace." But of course there is no "peace"—the war only manifests the general human condition. "They" will get you in Switzerland as well as Italy.

Our misgivings about Frederic's affair with Catherine can be traced, then, to the fictional world of *A Farewell to Arms*. But the premonition of disaster is also implicit in the novel's narrative structure. The novel's pattern is cyclical, as Frederic's fortunes alternately rise and fall. Book 1 charts Frederic's descent into the horrors of war. In book 2 his fate improves radically once he is taken to Milan, where he consummates his affair with Catherine. But book 3 returns Frederic to the front, where everything is worse than before. In book 4 and early in book 5, the happiness of Milan emerges again, as Frederic and Catherine make their escape to Switzerland. But just as the interlude in Milan was cut short, to be followed by a change for the worse, so the interlude in Switzerland is abbreviated. The pattern is such that we must anticipate this, despite the apparent serenity of life in Switzerland. We must recall what has happened to a similar "bliss" in Milan. In Milan, Frederic's memories of the war have been exorcised in his affair with Catherine. But soon the rains come, heralding the end of this idyll. Summer passes into fall, and the lovers' happiness passes with the season. First there is Catherine's premonition about the rain: "I'm afraid of the rain because sometimes I see me dead in it." This is followed by Catherine's discovery that she is pregnant, Frederic's bout with jaundice, the cancellation of his leave, and their last night in a hotel, where Catherine feels like a whore. Interspersed are reflections such as Frederic's on Catherine's pregnancy: "You always feel trapped biologically." And at the hotel Frederic is made to quote "To His Coy Mistress" on the pressure of Time's winged chariot. Thus the Milan interlude dwindles into an ominous prelude to book 3. When Frederic and Catherine revive their love in Switzerland, we must expect a similar "worsening" in their fate. And death is the one fate worse than the Caporetto retreat.

The devices used to mark this decline in happiness illustrate Hemingway's general use of omens. As much as anything else, these omens account for our tragic expectations. The most famous omen is of course the rain, which accompanies every disaster in the book, from the marching of the soldiers in the first chapter to the night of Catherine's death. But other omens are plentiful. They range from literary allusions to the real blood which drips on Frederic after he is wounded. A few prepare for specific events, as when the Italians talk about the carabinieri shooting every tenth man in an army which refused to fight. We will see this practice again, as applied to Frederic himself. And the nightmare of the retreat is prefaced by more than dreary weather. Frederic returns from the hospital to a unit far advanced into despair. The major's "it has been bad" is like a fateful echo; the mess hall that was boisterous is now almost empty; and Rinaldi's depression is more fearful than anything else, for his cynicism had seemed an impregnable defense. As conditions in the unit prepare for the ultimate deterioration of the retreat, so the final disaster of Catherine's death is specifically anticipated. Just before she is to give birth, we learn that Catherine is "narrow" in the hips. And this leads to a second paraphrase of the Marvell poem: "We knew the baby was very close now and it gave us both a feeling as though something were hurrying us and we could not lose any time together."

Thus tragic expectations are raised throughout the novel, by means of Frederic's meditations, the foreboding events and narrative structure, and the unabashed use of omens. These expectations are of course satisfied. Catherine's death has been much criticized as basically gratuitous. But it is gratuitous only if judged by everyday expectations. In the novel itself, as Carlos Baker has said, "Catherine's dying is directly associated with the whole tragic pattern of fatigue and suffering, loneliness, defeat and doom, of which the war is itself the broad social manifestation." Moreover, Catherine's death is appropriate for the effect Hemingway desired. *Because* she is not destroyed through her own actions, or Frederic's, or even by the war, Catherine's fate is generalized. Hemingway insists on the tragedy of life itself, not merely the insanity of war. And this is embodied, for the last time, in the manner of Catherine's death.

But we have come full circle, for the skeptical will reply that if Hemingway embodies his view of life in Catherine's death, this view is not tragic. How can a death so arbitrary, so "accidental," produce a tragic effect? Why are the expectations I have discussed tragic? The answer surely lies in what we come to feel toward Frederic and Catherine. To move us with the force of tragedy, Hemingway had to present his hero and heroine as something more than "victims," poor worm-like figures whose fate might inspire pity but not fear. Yet in a very real sense, of course, Frederic and Catherine *are* victims. And surely they are not "responsible" for what happens to them. How, then, can we respond to their fate as genuinely heroic? We do so, I think, because Hemingway has portrayed his lovers in the one light which makes the tragedy possible. Unlike Romeo and Juliet—or Willy Loman, for that matter—Frederic and Catherine are not portrayed as moral innocents; they are very much aware of the unjust world which victimizes them. Their decision to love is a conscious choice, made without illusions. Ultimately, this makes all the difference in how we respond to their fate.

As others have pointed out, Frederic is presented from the first as an *initiate*, in Hemingway's sense of the term. (It is seldom acknowledged that Catherine is Frederic's equal in this respect. She is far from innocent when they first meet. She is aware that Frederic's first advances are casual, perhaps cynical, with a "nurse's-evening-off aspect." She would not have them "lie" to each other. In fact, Catherine is fairly tough-minded. Her first lover was killed, she tells Frederic, and that was the end of it. "I don't know," Frederic replies. "Oh, yes," she says. "That's the end of it.") The ties which Stephen Dedalus once rejected—family, church, and state—are equally impossible in the world of this novel. Frederic is so reticent about his family that even Catherine must finally ask, "Have you a father?" Only at page 314 do we learn that Frederic and his family have "quarrelled"; otherwise, we are told almost nothing of his background. What this implies is complete estrangement from his past, his American heritage. With all of this he is disillusioned. It is much the same with religion. We are constantly reminded that both Frederic and Catherine are unbelievers. And Frederic is disillusioned with society no less than with his family or religion. The "order" of society has been unmasked by the war society has conspired to make. We see this in the conversation between Frederic and his Italian subordinates just before they are blown up. The Italians are extremely cynical about their country's "cause" and those who advance it most vigorously (the carabinieri). "You should not let us talk this way, Tenente," Passini tells Frederic. But Frederic cannot silence what he is coming to believe himself. Later, his remarks on the war will echo Passini's.

Frederic's disillusionment is crucial because it bears directly on his affair with Catherine. The affair begins as a wartime diversion, a game of seduction which Frederic likens to the games of chess and bridge. Of course, Frederic and Catherine are quickly beyond this first stage of their love. So quickly, in fact, that one side to the affair is often underestimated. After he first makes love to Catherine, Frederic thinks, "God knows I had not wanted to fall in love with her. I had not wanted to fall in love with any one." This agrees with the little we know of Frederic's past. Certainly he would fear the consequences of loving anyone in the world he has known. Frederic generalizes for us what the novel's action everywhere confirms, that "abstract words such as glory, honor, courage, or hallow were obscene beside the concrete names of villages, the numbers of roads, the names of rivers, the numbers of regiments and the dates"— obscene because unreal, untrue. "Love" is not included in this list, but what we call love can be just as "obscene" as glory, honor, or courage.

So it is meaningful when Frederic finally commits himself to what is akin to these values. Of course, what he gives himself to is love in the flesh, something as concrete as the name of a river. But it is a remarkable conversion nonetheless. The initiate who goes to Milan and its "exciting" nights, the man we first meet in a brothel, the man who tells Catherine he has never loved anyone—it is this man who finally commits his whole life to one woman. Because Frederic is at first so suspicious, even cynical, the ensuing love affair is all the more impressive. Only by developing the affair in this way could Hemingway be sure of our sympathy and respect. We sympathize with his lovers because they are fully aware of the dangers they court, yet choose to love anyway. Indeed, we do more than sympathize. We come to see their affair as the one positive value in an alien world. In the absence of conventional religious beliefs, Frederic and Catherine discover what Count Greffi defines as the human equivalent of religious faith: "Then too you are in love. Do not forget that is a religious feeling." This is the one valid faith in *A Farewell to Arms;* it is so important *because* it is the one valid faith.

Ironically, this is what makes possible the full tragic force of the novel's ending. Formally speaking, Hemingway elicits our sympathy so that he can generate the tragic emotion which pervades *A Farewell to Arms*. For if we admire the lovers' courage, we must recall what Frederic tells us about such courage: "If people bring so much courage to this world the world has to kill them to break them, so of course it kills them." We come to believe in the man who speaks here, so we must anticipate his own "breaking." As in all tragedies, the power of *A Farewell to Arms* derives from the tension between what we desire for its hero and what we *know* will be his fate. Hemingway establishes his fictional world as more or less what Frederic thinks it to be (a world which breaks and kills indiscriminately, where nothing is sacred). Everything in the novel justifies Frederic's most severe view of this world, which is tragic if not nihilistic. At the same time, everything contributes to our feeling that Frederic's values are exemplary, his love for Catherine nothing less than noble. In brief, everything contributes to form the tragedy of a perfectly admirable course of action, which we must desire, inevitably ending in catastrophe, which we must always anticipate.

Once he had achieved these conditions, Hemingway had surely made a formal tragedy. Indeed, he had made an innovation in the form. The "mistaken" actions of the hero have nothing to do with his fate, unless we would perversely judge Frederic for choosing to love Catherine. The assumption underlying this tragedy is that the enemy is not only within— it is also out there, in the universe itself. In a sense, it *is* the universe, that dark and destructive context for all that happens in *A Farewell to Arms*. This is consistent, of course, with much modern thought. There is really no reason why it should not be the basis for modern art as well—even tragic art. Sophocles himself, in the most famous of tragedies, portrayed a hero "victimized" by the nature of his world. Yet Oedipus remains the agent in his downfall, the one who murders his father and marries his mother. Even Hardy and Conrad retain this role for their tragic heroes. Hemingway has shown that this is not necessary in at least some versions of tragedy. We can continue to argue that no such tragedy is possible, because moral responsibility is indispensable to the form. But the emotional impact of *A Farewell to Arms* argues otherwise.

A Farewell to Arms:
A Dream Book

William Adair

Of Hemingway's fiction in general, Malcolm Cowley writes that it has "a waking-dreamlike quality," that it presents "nightmares at noonday, accurately described, pictured without blur, but having the nature of obsessions or hypnagogic visions between sleep and waking." This essay is in a sense a detailed footnote on Cowley's important observations, an attempt to get at what we might call the mechanics that make *A Farewell to Arms* Hemingway's "dream book."

Other of Hemingway's fictions suggest a dream analogy. Much of *The Sun Also Rises* comes over like a vivid enervating dream, and *Across the River and into the Trees* has a charged and sensitized atmosphere that implies that the story transpires in another country, a country for which the metaphor "dream" seems as appropriate as any. And among the short stories the quality of a waking dream seems especially pertinent to "A Way You'll Never Be," "Now I Lay Me," and as Cowley shows us, "Big Two-Hearted River." It is significant that all of these stories are played out in the shadow of a traumatic wounding, and that the wounding recurs in the dreams of the protagonists. This wounding is given fictional embodiment in *A Farewell to Arms*. And so it is not surprising to find that in this book Hemingway's fiction comes closest to the condition of a dream.

Perhaps it has not been sufficiently recognized that each of Hemingway's major books is a kind of new direction, and not only as a literary type (romantic tragedy, epic, fable, etc.) but also stylistically; and further,

From *The Journal of Narrative Technique* 5, no. 1 (January 1975). © 1975 by Eastern Michigan University Press.

that the "style" is intimately related to the "type." Our purpose here is to identify the type and consequent style of *A Farewell to Arms,* to identify those aspects of structure and style that are fundamental in determining the "dream condition" of the book: abstract methods more characteristic of romance literature, and romance literature's dark and excessive congeners, expressionism and surrealism, than of realism or symbolic naturalism, the usual categories for Hemingway's style. To provide a simplifying analogy: the book is somewhat closer to one of those dark and chaotic (or better, alternately light and dark) nineteenth-century romances, such as Melville's *Pierre,* to Strindberg's dream plays and the lucid nightmares of Kafka's novels than it is to the symbolic realism found, for instance, in the short fiction of Chekhov and Joyce.

Geometry, the psychology of repetition, and genre. These three perspectives will provide our primary approaches to the book, and so it may be helpful to begin with a few general comments on their relevance.

Defending *Across the River* against the harsh judgments of the reviewers, Hemingway said, "In writing I have moved through arithmetic, through plane geometry and algebra, and now I am in calculus. If they don't understand that, to hell with them." This mathematical analogy obviously has to do with the centripetal relationship among words in a fictive context, though beyond this it is somewhat mysterious. But assuming Hemingway intended this as a serious piece of descriptive criticism (and I suspect he did), it is tempting to see the "geometry and algebra" phase exemplified in *A Farewell to Arms.* Algebra deals with "symbols" that "stand for numbers: it is used esp. in the solution of polynominal equations": e.g., dust + rain + falling leaves = doom; "addition and multiplication are replaced by general binary operations": e.g., mountains + plains = home + not-home. Carlos Baker (who focuses rather exclusively on "general binary operations") has done quite a bit with the "algebra" of the book. One of our interests here is in its "geometry": those aspects of structure and style that help create an atmosphere of dream, and usually of nightmare.

Geometry [according to Webster's] deals with "points, lines, planes, and solids, and examines their properties, measurements, and mutual relations in space." As we shall see, in the most frightening parts of the book place description takes on an intensely geometric-linear character; and this predominantly linear creation of place gives long sections of the book a surrealistic and dreamlike ambience. Somewhat like the markedly geometric character of place in the novels of Alain Robbe-Grillet, the retreat from Caporetto and the final scene at the hospital in Lausanne are in a sense geometric nightmares: an intense nighttime and nightmare action that suggests bondage and frustration, depicted against a geometrized (and hence internalized) landscape. And there are several movements or actions that are structurally ("relations in space") identical; this repetition of a prototypical action, an action that culminates in a "breaking," renders the frightening and compulsive character of a familiar nightmare.

Philip Young's trauma theory provides another and I am sure a less debatable approach to the dream character of the book. Beginning with Freud's idea that the dreams of trauma victims obey a repetition compulsion, Young argues that the unmastered amounts of excitement caused by Hemingway's wounding at Fossalta di Piave resulted in the need for fictional returns to scenes of violence as a way of mastering the effects of this traumatic experience. Young sees this as a general condition of Hemingway's fiction. Our interest is restricted to *A Farewell to Arms.* The book is a nightmare emotion (fear of death) "recollected" in what is apparently a kind of stoic tranquillity. But more than a remembrance, it is a compulsive and repetitive reexperiencing of things past; or as the wounding (and consequently, the subsequent action) has the estranging quality of a dream, it is a fictional redreaming. The nightmare of the wounding—the book's prototypical action—is presented three times (spring, fall, spring), three instances that are *structurally* identical; the action is redreamed until the fear of death is exorcised, "mastered," in the death of Catherine, in the death of Frederic's other self.

The lyric impulse predominates in this book, and the lyric impulse extended and embodied in what is usually a relatively simple plot is literature in the romance mode. And so it is appropriate that the fortunes of Frederic and Catherine are closely allied to the calendar, thus suggesting the faint outlines of ritual action. Here Northrop Frye can help with another perspective on the book's dream structure. "Ritual is not only a recurrent act, but an act expressive of a dialectic of desire and repugnance. . . . In dream there is a parallel dialectic, as there is both the wish-fulfillment dream and the anxiety or nightmare dream of repugnance" (*Anatomy of Criticism*).

A Farewell to Arms presents this dialectic of eros and thanatos. The "dream image" (writ large) of thanatos is presented three times: the spring, the fall, and the concluding spring sections of the book. And these three dream images are essentially the *same* image: not only do they present what is structurally the same action, but they do so in the same dark atmosphere, and to the accompaniment of the same imagery: images of fragmentation and geometric-linear images. The "dream image" of eros is presented twice: in the summer and winter (i.e., "daylight") sections of the book. And they too are much the same, in terms of action, mood, and imagery.

The simplest way to proceed is to present in turn—spring, summer, fall, winter, spring—these two dream images, this dialectic of the dark and the light.

I. SPRING, 1917

In a sense the opening section *is* the nightmare reality; the fall and final spring sections "structural" reenactments of the nightmare; and the summer and winter sections erotic dreams that are escapes from the nightmare. But as the entire story has about it a dreamlike character, it seems correct to say that this opening spring section suggests a quality, if not of nightmare, then one of impending nightmare. It is all preparatory and leading up to the violence of the wounding, a violence which is not unlike the concluding event of a nightmare: sudden and "unreasonable"—unmerited, and given Frederic's war-in-the-movies attitude, illogical—and at once a surprise and known ahead of time. It is a surprise to the protagonist-as-actor, known ahead of time by the narrator-as-dreamer; known, but as in a dream, over which he has no control. And this foreknowledge, and in a sense, "fear," of the wounding presides over the selection of imagery, action, dialogue, mood, etc.: e.g., the flashes in the night from artillery in the mountains, strife among the officers, drunken nights and whirling rooms, the attempted seduction "in the dark" of a girl who is "a little crazy" and thus unpredictable, the fear of being on the edge of a war that may never end; and generally, a feeling of boredom and repetition and a sense of things running down and out of control. These are all conditions that imply the possibility of a sudden "explosion," and thus they are all prefaces to the wounding that the narrator knows is coming. His foreknowledge also determines the tone of this opening section: dark, tense, and meditative, and thus estranged, and in a sense, dreamlike. When Frederic is wounded his innocence is lost. When he is wounded, thoroughly and completely wounded, he falls out of his young dream of invincibility (war in the movies) and into the shadow of the constant threat of death.

This first section is a "dark" image, and so it is appropriate that the action begins with the sun being obscured by a cloud in the late afternoon, and that most of the action takes place at night and indoors. This nighttime and enclosed atmosphere implies a claustrophobic and interiorized (mental) world. It provides a correlative for the dominance of emotion over intellect: the temporal and subjective over the spatial, objective, and visual. Emotions are related to time and change; and time and change are "uncontrollable." The intellect is identified with the spatial, the timeless, and hence the seemingly controllable. Thus it is important to note that not only does the first section take place almost entirely at night, but that it transpires in the spring; and spring (like fall, and unlike summer and winter) is a season of change rather than a static season. It is the frightening passage of time, time that is leading to inevitable and uncontrollable violence—the wounding, the near-execution, the death of Catherine—that causes much of the tension in the story. And during the three dark sections of the book, time is on the move and so it is constantly threatening. The "light" sections suggest a continual present tense, an unchanging and erotic dreamworld wherein time and mutability have no power.

The major "change" that the first part of the book leads to is the wounding of the protagonist. The wounding is the primordial psychological event of the story, and it occurs, significantly, at night and underground. These nighttime and subterranean conditions suggest bondage, lack of control, and an estranged atmosphere—all characteristic of nightmare. More important, the scene implies a metaphoric descent into the dark regions of the mind for a momentary confrontation with death. The wounding establishes the protagonist's dominant emotion— the fear of death; and because the book is a redreaming of this event for the sake of mastery, the wounding provides the book's prototypical action, an action that may be outlined as follows:

(1) it begins with a separation from Catherine (in the opening section the separation takes place at the hospital in the late afternoon);

(2) a trip to the place of the violent "breaking" (the trip to the front); and on an equally important level, a journey from day into night and nightmare action;

(3) a meal with companions, a meal described in some detail (the spaghetti and cheese Frederic and his men share in the dugout);

(4) the sudden and unreasonable breaking (the explosion and wounding);

(5) departure from the place of the breaking.

When this action-paradigm reappears in the autumn and spring sections of the book, and reappears against a landscape—an interior landscape—characterized first by fragmentation, followed by an intensely linear creation of place, it suggests the frightening quality of a familiar nightmare, reenacted on familiar terrain. And thus it seems an extreme instance of the sensation Jake Barnes (who has his dreams, and probably war dreams) describes as "the feeling as in a nightmare of it all being something repeated, something I had been through and that now I must go through again . . . a feeling of things coming that could not be prevented."

Interior landscape: landscape characterized by "death" images of fragmentation and the surreal geometric-linear imagery that becomes so pronounced prior to violent disruption. This is interior and nightmare imagery not only because of its intrinsic connotations, but also because it is associated with the prototypical and nightmare action, and reappears when this action recurs. It is landscape that has remained in what Colonel Cantwell calls the "dreaming part of the mind."

Freud thought of death in terms of a disintegration and return to the elements. In Hemingway's fictional worlds we find something similar: images ("counters" for emotions) of fragmentation are death-images. The debris-strewn battlefields seen by Nick, and similarly, the battle sites described in "A Natural History of the Dead" suggest this value: broken houses and roads, corpses covered with flies and surrounded by scattered paper and weapons and ammunition, bodies blown to "fragments," fragments that are "found a considerable distance away in the fields." Nick's middle-aged avatar, Dick Cantwell, says that death comes not only with a "great white-hot, clanging roar," but also it "comes to you in small fragments that hardly show where it has entered."

In *A Farewell to Arms* the protagonist's constant fear of death is metaphorically expressed in the ultimate and final "breaking" (fragmenting) that haunts the book. And as the story is told in retrospect, it is a fear that is embedded in the imagery and implied in the dialogue even before the shattering wound is sustained. The book's fragmentation-imagery is not only imagery stored in the "dreaming part of the mind," but it is also (and the facts are connected) a matter of perception. Frederic tends to *see* his fear of death in a broken and piecemeal world, a world of thanatos, out of control and threatening. The spring section begins (as do the fall and final spring sections) with images of fragmentation: the falling leaves, the dust, even the rain and the dead (and numbered) troops of the opening chapter; the mountainside, which had been green during the previous summer, is now reduced to "stumps and broken trunks and the ground torn up"; the "broken houses of the town that was to be taken."

The breaking-motif receives its first "statement" the first evening Catherine and Frederic meet, in a sestet on the theme of "cracking," initiated by Catherine's remark about her former lover: "'They blew him all to bits'"; and concluding with her statement, "'Anyone may crack.'" Shortly afterward Frederic hopes the Austrians will "crack"; the disastrous retreat is caused by what is several times referred to as the "breaking of the line"; and of course there is Frederic's famous statement, "The world breaks everyone." The concluding "statement" of the breaking theme comes in the final section, during the "breaking-up of winter," as Catherine is nearing death. "'I'm all broken. They've broken me. . . . They just keep it up till they break you.'"

As the moment of violence approaches, Frederic's vision of the world changes from one of fragmentation to one cast in geometric-linear terms. Perhaps this geometrizing (interiorizing) of place reflects the protagonist's unconscious desire to "spatialize" time, to slow down and control the passage of time which is leading to the scene of violent change; perhaps it is a correlative for the protagonist's unspoken fear, and a stylistic device intended to arouse in the reader a similar state of fear and tension, and further, to make the shock of the breaking emotionally more "real" for the reader; or maybe the protagonist just happened to notice these "lines" on the trip to the place of the wounding and so they become associated with the action-paradigm.

During the trip to the front, the "journey from day into night and nightmare," Frederic sees (and sees in perspective) roads lined by trees, columns of troops, trucks, and guns, the river and the line of the railway tracks running beside the river. To give a suggestion of the density of linear imagery here, we can note that the word "road," chief among these several images, is used some twenty times in three pages. As we shall see, preludes to the subsequent breakings are much more intensely geometrized.

The wounding seems to return the world to fragments. Flashing lights often accompany the climax of a nightmare; and so it is worth noting that the "breaking" is preceded by and accompanied by flashing lights: a cigarette-lighter flashing in the dark, searchlights and bursting starshells outside the dugout, "then there was a flash, as when a blast-furnace door is swung open": the explosion and wounding. The explosion is followed by "brick and dirt *raining* down" (italics added) and "fragments of falling bricks"; and the wound is the result of a burst of shrapnel that leaves numerous fragments of metal lodged in the protagonist's legs.

The "dream" characteristics of this opening section are not as pronounced as in the rest of the book—especially the fall and final spring movements—for here the protagonist-as-actor has yet to be initiated into the world of constant threat and death. Here we have the nightmarish reality that determines the structure of subsequent redreamings; and the penumbra of dream this section does attain is to be attributed to the narrator-as-dreamer's foreknowledge of the violence that is coming.

II. SUMMER, 1917

The Milan section begins on a sunny morning and concludes at night with Frederic's departure for the front; and most of the action is daytime action. Again, these factors suggest the visual and controllable. And because this section of the book takes place in summer, a "static" season, we have the feeling that time and change do not threaten. It is also worth noting that the summer action ("We had a lovely time that summer." . . . "The summer went that way") is rendered in a kind of generalized fashion, and this also implies the static and unchanging. This long season is presented in fifty pages, whereas the fall section, a single week of intense action (the retreat and the flight to Switzerland), is presented in seventy pages, and thus in a kind of detailed and nightmarish "close-up."

Summer in Milan is a dream image of eros, a romance dream that is an escape from nightmare, and it is described in terms familiar to romance literature. Frederic and Catherine are in a sense archetypes, emotional attitudes embodied rather than "real" people: libido (wounded) and anima figures made flesh; and they are surrounded by benevolent parent-figures or spirits-of-place and a few "dark" characters who offer no real threat. Summer in Milan is a season of warm days of a somewhat miraculous convalescence, presided over by the somewhat miraculous Dr. Valentini (an appropriate name for a romance), Dr. Valentini of the animated mustaches and the prominent star. It is a summer of afternoon rides in the park in a carriage, walks about the city, and trips to the racetrack, where the dark forces of evil (those "dark" parent-figures, Meyers and his wife) are easily defeated by the forces of love. In the evenings our hero and heroine dine at a charming restaurant, where George, the headwaiter, is suddenly and rather inexplicably a close and helpful friend—not unlike the helpful spirits-of-place of medieval romance—knowledgeable in such nature-lore as the best wine-growing countries, who saves Frederic and his "lady" a table, selects their meals for them, and gladly lends Frederic a hundred lire. "'If you and the lady need money I've always got money.'" And their typical day is followed by cool and dreamlike nights of love, presented in appropriately brief and vague terms. It is a static world, controlled and bound together by the power of Eros.

The imagery of this section of the novel is not exaggerated (e.g., no images of fragmentation or passages of intensely linear imagery) but is objective, controlled, and "sane." If we can compare the spring, fall, and concluding spring sections of the book to paintings: the receding and perspective lines of Dali's daytime dreamscapes, followed by the night-scenes of flashing lights and sudden violence of Goya; then the "light" sections of the book, summer and winter, seem comparable to the solid and objective landscapes of Cézanne.

III. FALL, 1917

With the beginning of autumn, the nightmare begins again. Frederic leaves Catherine in Milan and reenters the world of time and change. "'But at my back I always hear / Time's winged chariot hurrying near'"—an appropriate sentiment for fall, a season of flight from time and death. And again, as in the spring section, this dark part of the book takes place chiefly at night: in the officers' mess, the rather slow beginning of the retreat, the last and most intense part of the retreat, and the night-flight up the lake to Switzerland. The retreat is the longest single action of his dark "dream image," and it provides the clearest and most extended instance of what we are calling the interior landscape of nightmare. Endured away from the dream of Catherine, it is suffered within the claustrophobic confines of the frightened and isolated mind; and thus it is presented in terms that approximate a surrealistic dreamscape, a geometric nightmare of bondage and repetition.

On one level the nightmare sensation of panicked and frustrated flight is achieved by what might be termed standard devices for the dark side of a romance. The whole countryside is on the move, attempting to flee along a single road that is intermittently blocked by stalled vehicles. One of Frederic's three trucks is stuck in the mud in the attempt to back out of a blind road. There are various unhelpful spirits-of-place; as in Kafka's novels, the nameless representatives of the dark They that await off-stage: the two sergeants who refuse to aid in getting the truck back in motion, and later, the "questioners," the anonymous executing officers of the beautiful detachment; the continual threat of enemy planes from overhead (seen three times), and enemy troops, pursuing from behind like Jungian shadow figures; and when the Germans are seen up close, it is the dreamlike apparition of the bicycle troops moving silently, "smoothly, almost supernaturally" across the bridge. And constantly, there is the threat of Time's winged vehicle, hurrying near, coming from behind, as is the enemy and death. "We walked along together all going fast against time."

Repetition of the structural paradigm established in the first section of the book suggests the dreamlike sensation of things coming that cannot be prevented. Faint outlines of the original traumatic event are discernible in the series of actions that begins with (1) the separation from Catherine in Milan; (2) followed by the return trip to the front; (3) the meal in the messhall with the officers; (4) and then the "breaking of the line" that results in the sudden shock of the retreat; (5) and then departure from the place of breaking, the retreat itself.

But it is better to see this action-series as a kind of foreshadowing of the more intense repetition of our ur-paradigm that follows. This more intense and detailed repetition begins shortly after the start of the retreat, as Frederic awakens from his dream of Catherine. (1) As the final words of the dream suggest (Frederic: "You wouldn't go away in the night would you?" Catherine: "Of course I wouldn't go away. I'm always here."), the Milan separation from Catherine is in a sense restated in the dream (when he awakens), in the middle of the night, and immediately before the retreat becomes suddenly dangerous; (2) this is followed by the most frightening part of the retreat, and it is a journey that proceeds from day into night and nightmare; (3) toward the conclusion Frederic shares a meal in the barn with his companions; (4) this is followed by the "breaking" of the arrest and near-execution; (5) and then departure from the scene of violence, the desertion.

As in the spring section of the book, the autumn section begins with images of fragmentation, interior and nightmare images that are death-images, suggesting a world that is broken and out of control. Returning to Gorizia, Frederic sees a world in fragments: "many houses had been hit." Later in the mess there is talk of eating the flesh of dead Austrians, "uncontrollable" industrial accidents, and Rinaldi's assumed sickness ("'A little pimple. . . . Then we notice nothing at all'"). And then again: "the road ended in a wrecked village"; the Austrians have been shelling the road, and "the fragments from the burst were enormous"; Frederic had not realized the Bainsizza "was so broken up"; "There were many iron shrapnel balls in the rubble of the houses and on the road beside the broken house where the post was." And of course this is followed by the "breaking of the line" that forces the retreat, and the retreat itself, an uncontrolled and scattered rout, which during the night is carried out under a constant rain.

As the moment of violence (the arrest) approaches, Frederic again sees the world in geometric-linear terms, and this time to a degree that implies a surrealistic dreamscape. This intensely linear and perspective creation of place begins (as do so many of Kafka's waking nightmares) almost immediately after the protagonist awakens from sleep, in the morning after he awakens from his dream of Catherine; and continues until he is on the flatcar, under the canvas tarp, on his way back to Milan and Catherine.

During the retreat, during the day that precedes the night of violent breaking, Frederic seems caught up in a geometric maze that implies the nightmare sensation of vulnerability and arrested flight; a proliferation of advancing and receding, crossing and paralleling lines: low stone walls running across fields, railway tracks, canals, a river spanned by a series of stone bridges, and, especially, *roads* ("We had worked through a network of secondary roads and had taken many roads that were blind, . . ."), roads lined by hedges, ditches, and trees. This geometric-linear imagery is often given a suggestion of the surreal by the seeing-eye-protagonist's "perspective" renditions: looking up, but most frequently, looking back down the lines of roads (as if fearing the approach to time and death), river, tracks, etc.

Again, we can get an idea of the intensely linear (and interior) character of place during the retreat by noticing that the word/image "road" appears some fifty times in ten pages; and thereafter until the desertion (another fifteen pages) it appears twenty-seven times. The second most frequently used linear image is "bridge," and it too is most often seen in perspective.

There is another mode of repetition here that helps create the sensation of a familiar nightmare. Hemingway is essentially a lyric writer; thus his basic impulse is to express, to find correlatives for, his vision rather than to re-create the "real world." This means that *A Farewell to Arms* is constructed out of emotional "counters," the selection and arrangement of which is presided over by a dominant emotion (fear of death). Landscape, action, weather, time (mountains and plains, nighttime flights from violence, rain, clear cold mornings, Time's winged vehicle)—and as we have seen, characters as archetypes—are counters to be used in rendering the dominant emotion; or, extended and complicated, the personal vision of the lyric writer. Earl Rovit argues that because of this lyric tendency Hemingway's fictional worlds are first of all places of the mind, out of "real" space and time: "enclosed and removed, existentially rootless as surreal landscapes in which the reader and the narrator (overt or covert) may share in their inward reality."

Richard Cantwell says, "'We live by accidents of terrain, you know. And terrain is what remains in the dreaming part of the mind.'" He might have been providing a gloss on *A Farewell to Arms*. For the essential features of landscape during the retreat, those aspects of terrain that have remained in the dreaming part of the protagonist's mind—roads, river, railway tracks, stone bridges, stone farmhouses and low stone walls running across fields—are the *same* that made up the place description during the trip to the front that ended in the traumatic wounding. Thus during the retreat these images or emotionally significant counters take on a kind of *déjà vu* quality—not unlike the house, stable, and canal of Nick's recurring nightmare in "A Way You'll Never Be"—creating an especially compelling atmosphere, as it is the landscape of a recurring nightmare.

IV. WINTER, 1917–18

As the fall section of the book ends at night with the flight up the lake to Switzerland, so the winter section begins, structurally, in the morning, after the nightmare is over, as they disembark in Switzerland. The action of this section takes place almost entirely in the daytime; and of course the winter is, like summer, a long season without change, a static season.

There are other suggestions that their summer in Milan, an erotic dream, is now being redreamed in Switzerland—that it is the *same* dream. Frederic's and Catherine's activities are "structurally" much the same as they were during the summer: walking the roads and walking the streets of the town, and after they descend to Lausanne, riding out in a carriage, and for Frederic, daily workouts at the gym, much like his daily exercising at the Ospedale Maggiore in Milan. And the winter action ("We had a fine life.") is presented chiefly in a generalized fashion, again suggesting the static and unchanging: the long winter season is rendered in about as many pages as is the final scene (and chapter) at the hospital, which is a day and a half (as was the retreat), and presented in the close-up and oppressive detail of nightmare.

Isolated atop a snowy mountain in " 'a country where nothing makes any difference,' " winter in Switzerland is a romance dream, a dream world wherein Catherine and Frederic " 'never see anyone' " and so are in a sense lord and lady of their own "interior" kingdom. (It is of course Frederic's interior world, Frederic's dream.) It is a country of romance where newborn babies would seem out of place; where war is like a football game at someone else's college; and where "they" (parents safely ensconced in a distant land) honor all sight drafts. Walking out into the enchanting winter forest, the hero and his lady encounter foxes (and imagine themselves with such fine and useful tails as the foxes have) and colorful local "nature" figures: the woodsmen (bearded, as is Frederic) and the chamois hunter of the legendary and semi-magical talents, or at least, talisman (the tiny gold earrings). And of course, back "home" there are those two "good parent" figures, Mr. and Mrs. Guttingen, always helpful, happy to serve breakfast in bed, unconcerned about such mundane matters as advance notice on the chalet (the hero and heroine depart suddenly when the rains come), who have sent their son to Zurich, where he is studying to become a headwaiter, as Mr. Guttingen himself had been, and doubtless, much in the line of the admirable George of Milan. This is a period in time (or out of time) that reaches a kind of ultimate of rest and stillness during the three weeks of heavy snow that restricts their activity. Or perhaps it is the penultimate of rest and stillness, death being the ultimate; which suggests that here eros and thanatos are drawing close together. Altogether there is again the suggestion that time and change have come to a temporary standstill.

As in the summer section, the imagery here is not exaggerated, but is as clear and firm and objective as a bright morning—a landscape by Cézanne rather than Dali (day) or Goya (night). But all of this begins to change when the three-day rains come ("In March came the first break in the weather.") turning the road to a torrent of muddy water and turning the snow to slush.

V. MARCH, 1918

With the approach of spring (a season of change) Catherine and Frederic return to the world of time and mutability. And true to the pattern of the "dark" sections, the description of action in this final section (the hospital scene) takes place almost entirely at night (and like the opening section, indoors). Again, these matters suggest the claustrophobic and interiorized; the dominance of emotion and lack of control over circumstances. Time is on the move, the third nightmare begins, and the final "breaking" is drawing nearer.

The estranged and dreamlike character of the hospital scene is suggested by a number of minor touches. Frederic is awakened at three in the morning (as he was during the retreat and before the flight up the lake to Switzerland); and again, he is awakened to the beginning of a nightmare; the frustrating delay in getting the cab company to answer the phone, followed by the delay in getting the hotel elevator in motion: on a structural level, both similar to the panic-situation of the stalled vehicles during the retreat; the strangeness of Catherine's voice because of the gas; Frederic returns from the cafe and is surprised to find Catherine's room "suddenly" empty, the doctor unrecognized in white cap and mask, and later the strange sight of himself in cap, gown, and beard; and the view of Catherine, who appears dead, below on the operating table of the amphitheater: "It looked like a drawing of the Inquisition."

The quality of a familiar nightmare is suggested by the third and final rendition of our structural paradigm, the third "compulsive return" to the scene of the traumatic experience; which again creates the frightening feeling of things coming that cannot be prevented: (1) a separation from Catherine as she goes in for the delivery; (2) followed by a "journey," Frederic's constant passage up and down the hallways; and on another level, it is the now familiar trip from day into night and nightmare; (3) Frederic has a meal with others at the cafe just prior to the end (the repetition of the action-paradigm may suggest to Frederic the urgency of returning to the hospital: "Suddenly I knew I had to get back."); (4) the "breaking" of Catherine, like the wounding and the arrest and near-execution, undeserved and unreasonable; (5) followed by Frederic's departure from the breaking-place, the walk back to the hotel.

Perhaps it is fair to say that this final dark movement also begins with images of fragmentation: the constant rain, the mud and slush of the "breaking-up of winter"; the coffee grounds, dust, and dead flowers found in the refuse cans along the street. And toward the end of this final section the imagery again becomes markedly linear, implying the nightmare approach of another breaking.

The chief linear image of "interior landscape" here is "hall" (and "hallway" and "corridor"), used repeatedly in this final chapter, and most often in the phrase "down the hall." In the final twenty pages of the book (interrupted by three trips "down the street" to the cafe) the words "hall," "hallway," and "corridor" are used thirty-three times; the word "hall" is used seventeen times in the dominant phrase of the chapter, "down the hall." During the retreat the protagonist seemed caught up in a geometric maze that suggested the nightmare sensation of arrested flight. In this final chapter Frederic is trapped within the geometry of hallways, a "bare hallway with two windows and closed doors all down the hall," as Catherine is dying within a series of closed rooms. His constant movement up and down the halls, especially, and also in and out of elevators, implies a claustrophobic ritual that is not only a correlative for his state of fear and tension, but also for the dreamlike sensation of powerlessness and the feeling that a recurring nightmare is coming to its conclusion and greatest intensity.

The repeated use of the word "hall" and the phrase "down the hall" (like the roads during the retreat, often viewed in perspective) in the final chapter tend not only to create a dreamlike, even a surrealistic mental landscape, but it again suggests a compulsive reiteration of a geometric aspect of place that occurs at earlier and, psychologically, important junctures of the novel. As the road, river, railway tracks, and stone bridges, walls, and farmhouses of the retreat seemed imbued with certain "dark" implications picked up during Frederic's trip to the place of the wounding; so the hall-image of the final chapter comes with certain connotations. It is an image that is an emotionally significant "counter," an image that "remains in the dreaming part of the mind." The word "hall" appears rather frequently within the closed field of the book, and most often in the phrase "down the hall." But the word and the expression are *first* used in association with the marble statuary that Frederic sees in the office and the hallway ("The hallway too . . . was lined with them.") as he waits for Catherine at the hospital that spring prior to the wounding. "I saw Catherine Barkley coming down the hall." And of course his remark, "marble busts all looked like a cemetery," gains considerable significance in relation to the final paragraph of the book: "It was like saying good-by to a statue."

The next two times the phrase "down the hall" appears it is associated with Catherine in an erotic manner. Shortly afterward (and very near to the time of the wounding) Frederic is again waiting for Catherine at the hospital in Gorizia. He hears someone "coming down the hall," and is disappointed to find that it is Miss Ferguson, who tells him that Catherine will not be able to see him as she is sick; and so Frederic leaves the hospital: "suddenly I felt lonely and empty . . . I was feeling lonely and hollow." At the conclusion of the book a nurse again tells him he cannot see Catherine as she is "sick." And when he leaves the hospital he once again feels empty and hollow and lonely—though this time the feeling is greatly intensified, and perhaps permanent.

There are other dream, or at least "interior," conditions we could mention: the frequent occurrence of revery and fantasizing, interior monologue, and "real" nightmares: Catherine's dream of seeing herself dead in the rain; Frederic's fear of nightmares keeps him from sleeping until dawn (this is after the wound and before he falls in love with Catherine); the story is presented in chiaroscuro (as are most people's dreams) rather than in color; the most intense action begins (as in Kafka) immediately after the protagonist has been awakened from sleep and concludes, as if it were in a dream, in the middle of the night. But all of these matters are peripheral to the book's central dream quality: the book gives us not an objective and continuous creation of the "real world," but an interior world that is a closed field of structural reenactment and stylistic repetition, a world, by turns, of the erotic imagination and the radically frightened mind. It is a dream world.

Hemingway once remarked, "The country that a novelist writes about is the country he knows; and the country he knows is in his heart." And the landscapes of this dark romance are geographies of the heart and the mind, "the dreaming part of the mind," a dreamscape across which the protagonist flees from time and death, reenacting the primordial event of the story (the wounding) until it is exorcised in the death of Frederic's other self, in the death of Catherine.

Going Back

Michael S. Reynolds

> *So we walked along through the street where I saw my very good friend killed,
> . . . and it all seemed a very sad business. I had tried to recreate something for
> my wife and had failed utterly. The past was as dead as a busted victrola
> record. Chasing yesterdays is a bum show—and if you have to prove it go back
> to your old front.*
>
> ERNEST HEMINGWAY, "A Veteran Visits Old Front" (*Toronto Star,* 22 July 1922)

When Frederic Henry, hero of Hemingway's *A Farewell to Arms,* lived in
the house "that looked across the river and the plain to the mountains,"
it was the late summer of 1915. Italy had just entered the European War,
and Ernest Hemingway had just turned sixteen in upper Michigan. In
the spring of 1918, Catherine Barkley died in childbirth in Lausanne,
Switzerland; in April 1918, Ernest Hemingway drew his last paycheck
from the *Kansas City Star* and left for his own war experience in northern
Italy.

When he reached Italy in 1918 for his shortlived tour as a Red Cross
ambulance driver, the Italian front bore no resemblance to the front at
which Frederic had served for two years as an ambulance driver in the
Italian army. In June 1918, American Red Cross Ambulance Section Four,
to which Hemingway was assigned, was stationed at Schio in the Dolomite foothills. Although there was a major Austrian offensive in June,
there was little action at Schio. Hemingway drove Section Four ambulances for only three weeks. In July he asked to be transferred to the
canteen operation along the more active Piave river front. At Fossalta di
Piave, on July 8, 1918, he was blown up by an Austrian trench mortar.

From *Hemingway's First War: The Making of* A Farewell to Arms. © 1976 by Princeton
University Press.

He had been in the war zone for about one month, and he was not to return to it actively in that war.

Carlos Baker has remarked that Hemingway was acutely conscious of *place,* and that he was painfully accurate in his geographic descriptions. Mary Hemingway has described the careful checking of street names and distances that Hemingway put into *A Moveable Feast.* Hemingway himself said that his concern was for "the way it was," which he loosely defined as "the people, the places, and how the weather was." Against this concern it is difficult to balance his lack of firsthand knowledge of the Italian front of 1915–17. He had not seen the Tagliamento river when he wrote *A Farewell to Arms;* he had not walked the Venetian plain between Codroipo and Latisana. It was not until 1948 that he saw Udine. He may never have seen Gorizia, the Isonzo river, Plava, or the Bainsizza plateau; he certainly had not seen them when he wrote the novel. His return trip to Fossalta di Piave in 1922 and his skiing trip at Cortina d'Ampezzo in 1923 did not take him to the terrain of the novel. His 1927 trip to Italy with Guy Hickock did not cover the war zone of 1915–17. Not only had Hemingway not experienced the military engagements in which Frederic Henry takes part, but he had not seen the terrain of books 1 and 3 of *A Farewell to Arms.* Yet the geography is perfectly accurate and done with the clarity that made its author famous for his descriptions of place.

Because the Caporetto section (book 3) is so powerfully written, most critics have confined their remarks about military descriptions to this portion of the book, being content to make generalizations about the remainder of the military activity in the novel. Book 3 has been widely recognized for its narrative excellence, and early reviewers like Malcolm Cowley, Percy Hutchinson, and H. S. Canby responded to Hemingway's power in this section. Canby called the description of the retreat a "masterly piece of *reporting*" (my emphasis). Yet none of these men had served on the Italian front and should not be expected to notice minor inaccuracies if they existed.

Later critics, more knowledgeable about Hemingway's biography, knew that he had not participated in the retreat; but they also knew that he had covered the Greek retreat in the Greco-Turkish War (1922) as a journalist. It was an easy assumption that Hemingway had transposed his Greek experience to the Friulian plain of northern Italy: steady rain, muddy roads, stumbling refugees. What this assumption fails to account for is the considerable amount of specific detail in book 3 of *A Farewell to Arms* that has nothing to do with muddy roads or refugees.

One would expect European readers to be more critical. Yet one

French reviewer wrote: "The one aspect of the last war which has least interested writers is the defeat. . . . There has been need for an American witness on the Alpine front who could reveal to us, in its abject horror, the Italian rout near Caporetto: . . . If Hemingway has not dedicated all his book to this debacle, . . . one can believe that he had to obey auto-biographical motives."

Italian critics, some of whom took part in the Caporetto retreat, were unable to find any fault with Hemingway's history or geography. The Italian fascist government under Mussolini found the account of Caporetto so painful, and presumably so accurate, that *A Farewell to Arms* was banned in Italy until after World War II. In 1930 one Italian reviewer saw the novel as unvarnished autobiography: "[The novel] narrates autobiographically his experience as an officer on the Italian front after he, although a foreigner, enlisted in our army as a volunteer, more through the desire to do like everyone else (he was already in Italy as an architecture student) than through ideological dedication; and then of his flight as a deserter after Caporetto . . . every page of the books resembles a sheet torn from a notebook. . . . One hears the eulogy of the Duke of Aosta pronounced in words so banal and nasty as to move anyone who remembers the Duke and those years at all well to protest . . . *the time is objectively precise, with references to dates and 'historical' episodes,* but it has no color, no duration . . . diary composition comes to mind . . . rather too scrupulous and unified" (my emphasis).

Twenty-five years later another Italian critic, reading the book more sympathetically and more nostalgically, was no less convinced of the historic and geographic accuracy: "Four-fifths of the work unfolds in Northern Italy, in Milan and above all among the hills, mountains and plains of the Veneto which are particularly dear to my heart. *Every landscape evoked in the now famous novel, every place cited, is familiar to me. . . . The novel . . . evokes the climate of the first two years of the war until the disaster of Caporetto with extraordinary vivacity. . . . All that his protagonist narrates has an undeniable sound of authenticity. . . .* After the intoxication of the days in May (*which he does not mention but in which he* [Hemingway] *certainly must have taken part to be led to enlist and leave for the front during his stay in Italy*) he found himself in a country in which the war was not felt but only submitted to as a calamitous circumstance . . . *this actually was . . . the climate of Italy between the summer of 1915 and the autumn of 1917. The picture painted by Hemingway is exact . . . one who wishes to know what the defeat was like in the minds of officers and soldiers of the Second Army after Caporetto can read* A FAREWELL TO ARMS. Perhaps in no other book are the tragic days relived with such intensity. . . . Only one who truly loves the country, who has suffered there and lived there intensely can describe the Venetian countryside, or speak of the disaster of Caporetto as Ernest Hemingway has done" (my emphasis).

In 1954 Alberto Rossi, who had collaborated on several translations of Hemingway novels into Italian, reviewed Charles Fenton's *The Apprenticeship of Ernest Hemingway*. Rossi reminded his Italian readers that Hemingway's considerable talents are above all "his ability to present a situation as actually lived with a few well-chosen touches; one tends instinctively to identify the character who narrates with the author himself, and thus to attribute to the author the intention of affirming, as authentic and experienced by him, all the details of his own story." But Rossi had great difficulty in believing that Hemingway had not taken part in the retreat from Caporetto: "That the work was in effect one of imagination and not of history, however evident this seems, was not an affirmation which could satisfy everyone's curiosity." He was perplexed by the accuracy he could not account for biographically: "It is no less evident that for certain parts of that novel his imagination was not working on data of direct experience; and among these is the impressive evocation of the retreat."

Even after Malcolm Cowley, in the introduction to the *Portable Hemingway,* pointed out that the author had not taken part in the Caporetto retreat, American critics failed to question Hemingway's accuracy. The main stream of Hemingway criticism has followed either Carlos Baker into romantic and biographic criticism or Philip Young into psychological analyses, all of which were encouraged by the virile public image Hemingway cultivated. One need only to read through the massive bibliography of Hemingway criticism to see how limited most second- and third-generation criticism has become and how debilitating it has been for the novels.

As early as 1922, Hemingway had begun to formulate a method of dealing with reality. In a feature story for the *Toronto Daily Star,* "A Veteran Visits Old Front," he told how depressing it was to return to the scene of battles he had taken part in, for the country was so changed that it ruined the memory. It would have been better to have visited a battle site he had not known: "Go to someone else's front if you want to. *There your imagination will help you out and you may be able to picture the things that happened*" (my emphasis). This same idea appears in the deleted coda to "Big Two-Hearted River" (ca. 1924):

The only writing that was any good was what you made up, what you imagined. . . . You had to digest life and then create your own people. . . . Nick in the stories was never himself. He had made him up. Of course he'd never seen an Indian woman having a baby. That was what made it good [my emphasis].

In a 1935 *Esquire* article Hemingway gave a somewhat fuller statement on the point:

Good writing is true writing. If a man is making a story up it will be true in proportion to the amount of knowledge of life he has and how *conscientious* he is; so that when he makes something up it is as it truly would be. . . . Imagination is the one thing beside honesty that a good writer must have, the more he learns from experience the more truly he can imagine. *If he gets so he can imagine truly enough people will think that the things he relates all really happened and that he is just reporting* [my emphasis].

In 1948, when he wrote his own introduction for an illustrated edition of *A Farewell to Arms,* Hemingway made no pretense of having experienced the historical events of the novel firsthand:

I remember living in the book and making up what happened in it every day. Making the country and the people and the things that happened I was happier than I had ever been. . . . Finding you were able to make something up; to create truly enough so that it made you happy to read it.

And in 1958, when he was interviewed by the *Paris Review,* Hemingway restated his position with the same simplicity he had used in 1922:

Q: Have you ever described any type of situation of which you had no personal knowledge?
A: That is a strange question. . . . A writer, if he is any good does not describe. *He invents or makes out of his knowledge personal and impersonal* [my emphasis].

Over a thirty-six-year span, Hemingway's attitude toward his profession remained constant on the point of "making it up." Yet no one ever took him very seriously, for he had been typed as an autobiographic writer when he published *The Sun Also Rises.* His statements about invented action on the basis of knowledge "personal and impersonal" appeared either simpleminded or some sort of ruse. They were neither.

In his terse disciplinary sketches written in 1922–23, Hemingway had already developed an objective style that treated the experience of others as his own. Of the eighteen sketches, called "chapters," collected in the 1924 edition of *in our time,* eight were based on second-hand information. Two of the sketches were based on the war experiences of his British friend, Captain E. E. Dorman-Smith, at the fighting around Mons. Another (chapter 16) described the goring and death of the matador Maera. At the time Hemingway had never seen a bullfight, and Maera was very much alive. Hemingway based his description on conversations with Mike Strater and Gertrude Stein. Chapter 6, which describes the inglorious execution of the deposed Greek cabinet ministers, was based on a newspaper clipping. The ninth chapter, which describes the shooting of the cigar-store bandits, was based on a story in the *Kansas City Star* from November 19, 1917. The hanging of Sam Cardinella (chapter 17) probably came from either police-station or city-room gossip from the Kansas City days. The description of the King of Greece in his garden (chap. 18) was based on information related to Hemingway by an acquaintance who had an informal interview with the king. From the beginning Hemingway felt free to use secondhand sources.

After Hemingway showered Stephen Crane with praise in his introduction to *Men at War,* critics began to note thematic and structural similarities between *The Red Badge of Courage* and *A Farewell to Arms.* What was carefully ignored by the critics was the reason why Hemingway said he admired Crane's novel:

> Crane wrote [*The Red Badge of Courage*] before he had ever seen any war. But he had read contemporary accounts, had heard the old soldiers, they were not so old then, talk, and above all he had seen Matthew Brady's wonderful photographs. Creating his story out of this material he wrote that great boy's dream of war that was to be truer to how war is than any war the boy who wrote it would ever live to see. It is one of the finest books in our literature and I include it entire because it is all as much of one piece as a great poem is.

Hemingway's praise is neither for Crane's structure nor for his theme; the praise is for the technique and the verity. In 1928, when he was writing his first war novel, Hemingway already knew about Crane's research method in *The Red Badge of Courage.* While working on the *Transatlantic Review* in 1924, Hemingway served as a sub-editor under

Ford Madox Ford. Ford had known Crane during the Brede Manor days in England, and later Ford both wrote and lectured on the young American writer. One of the things that Ford knew about Crane, and that was not public knowledge, was the way in which Crane had researched his war novel. During Hemingway's association with Ford in 1924, he must have heard the anecdote, probably more than once. Crane's research methods that Hemingway chose to praise—reading histories, talking to veterans, and looking at pictures—were the same methods that Hemingway used on *A Farewell to Arms*.

As early as 1922, Hemingway had already done sufficient historical reading to pose as an expert on a war in which he had served only briefly and that he later admitted he did not understand. When he wrote his *Toronto Daily Star* feature, "A Veteran Visits Old Front" (July 1922), he created the flat tone of the seasoned campaigner, alluding to many more events than he had experienced:

> I remember . . . looking out the window down at the road where the arc light was making a dim light through the rain. It was the same road that the battalions marched along through the white dust in 1916. They were the Brigata Ancona, the Brigata Como, the Brigata Tuscana and ten others brought down from the Carso, to check the Austrian offensive that was breaking through the mountain wall of the Trentino and beginning to spill down the valleys that led to the Venetian and Lombardy plains. They were good troops in those days and they marched through the dust of early summer, broke the offensive along the Gallo-Asiago-Canove line, and died in the mountain gullies, in the pine woods on the Trentino slopes, hunting cover on the desolate rocks and pitched out in the soft-melting early summer snow of the Pasubio.
>
> It was the same old road that some of the same brigades marched along through the dust in June 1918, being rushed to the Piave to stop another offensive. Their best men were dead on the rocky Carso in the fighting around Goritzia, on Mount San Gabrielle, on Grappa, and in all the places where men died that nobody ever heard about.

When he wrote those words Hemingway had never seen the Carso, Gorizia, or Mount San Gabrielle. When the road turned to dust at Schio in 1916, he was preparing for his senior year in high school. The journalist must always be the expert, and he had already developed a keen sense of the insider's information. He had learned that hard facts create an immediate sense of authenticity. Those were not just soldiers on any road—they were specific brigades who died at specific places. In order to write this article, Hemingway had done extensive reading on the art of war, which he continued throughout his life. He may not have known in 1922 how much he would need that reading in 1928 when he came to write *A Farewell to Arms,* but in the manuscript of the novel, historical facts, dates, places, and events roll from the writer's pencil with facility and accuracy.

In that 1922 visit to Schio, Hemingway realized a truth that he passed on to his readers and that he remembered when he tried to make fictional sense of his own war experience:

> Don't go back to visit the old front. If you have pictures in your head of something that happened in the night in the mud at Paschendaele, or of the first wave working up the slope of Vimy, do not try and go back and verify them. It is no good. The front is different from the way it used to be. . . . Go to someone else's front if you want to. There your imagination will help you out and you may be able to picture the things that happened. . . . The past was as dead as a busted victrola record. Chasing yesterdays is a bum show—and if you have to prove it go back to your old front.

If he functions in the realist/naturalist tradition, a writer is always chasing yesterdays. In writing *A Farewell to Arms,* however, Hemingway went back to someone else's front and recreated the experience from books, maps, and firsthand sources. It is his only novel set on terrain with which he did not have personal experience; in it, his imagination, aided by military histories, has recreated the Austro-Italian front of 1915–17 more vividly than any other writer.

Hemingway, the public man, may have been just as much of a romantic as some readers would see him, and many of his plots may have smelled of the museums, as Gertrude Stein thought. But as an artist, Hemingway was able to approach his material in those early years with an objectivity that never allowed personal experience or friendships to interfere with his fiction. Like most twentieth-century innovators, he found himself his own best subject, but to mistake his art for his biography is to mistake illusion for reality. In *Green Hills of Africa* no reader can believe that the dialogue is a reportorial account of what was actually said, or that there is no artistry in Hemingway's arrangement of the action. Even in *A Moveable Feast,* Hemingway warns the reader: "If the reader prefers, this book may be regarded as fiction. But there is always some chance that such a book of fiction may throw some light on what has been written as fact."

To read any of Hemingway's fiction as biography is always dangerous, but to read *A Farewell to Arms* in this manner is to misread the book. Hemingway himself was particularly anxious, during those early years, for Scribner's to keep biographical statements about him out of print. In letters to his editor, Max Perkins, he urged that the critics and readers be allowed to make up their own lies (February 14, 1927). He belittled his own war experiences, telling Perkins that the medals had been given to him simply because he was an American attached to the Italian army. One medal, he insisted, was awarded for action on Monte Maggiore when he was three hundred kilometers away in a hospital at the time. He did not want anyone to think him a faker, a liar, or a fool (February 19, 1929). Perkins agreed to correct misinformation that Scribner's had unknowingly given out to the media and to restrain the publicity department in the future, remarking that usually authors were so intent on such publicity that it had not occurred to him that Hemingway might be sensitive on the point.

Like most of his central characters, Hemingway in 1928–29 preferred to exist in the present tense, with as little reference to the past as possible, particularly his private past. Later, when biographical critics like Fenton and Young began to probe into his private life, Hemingway resented it bitterly. In a letter to Carlos Baker, he said that biographies of living writers were destructive in several ways. Because all writers wrote out of their own experience, the premature biographer was nothing more than a spoiler, ruining experiences that the writer might have turned into fiction. All writers, he insisted, write about living people; that is, they use them for the base upon which they build their fictional characters. Biographical critics were forcing him to create characters no longer credible because he had become so conscious of covering up the original.

Readers have always wanted to see the heroes as projections of their author, and critics have generally promoted the parallel. Hemingway, however, in the twenties never encouraged the parallelism. He admitted to using real prototypes for characters, like Cohn in *The Sun Also Rises,* but he felt that most of the characters he used did not read books. Unfortunately, *The Sun Also Rises* was read as a thinly veiled who's who of Paris and Pamplona, and Hemingway was never able to convince his critics afterwards that he did not do this all the time or that his central character was not himself. In 1926, he told Scott Fitzgerald that in spite of what he and Zelda always thought, "Cat in the Rain" was not a story about Hemingway and Hadley. He explained that the two characters were a Harvard graduate and his wife whom he had met in Genoa.

To read *A Farewell to Arms* as biography is to believe that Hemingway learned nothing from *The Torrents of Spring* and *The Sun Also Rises,* where the use of real people had caused him considerable difficulty. In the correspondence with Maxwell Perkins during the galley-proof stage of *The Sun Also Rises,* Perkins asked him to make numerous small changes to avoid libel suits. After much bargaining, Hemingway obscured references to Glenway Wescott, Hilaire Belloc, Joseph Hergesheimer, and Henry James. In *The Sun Also Rises* there is still a passing remark about "Henry's bicycle," which in the manuscript referred to Henry James's apocryphal groin injury similar to the one of Jake Barnes. Perkins advised Hemingway: "As for Henry James, you know how we feel about it . . . this town and Boston are full of people who knew him and who cannot regard him as you do, i.e. as an historical character. There are four right in this office who were his friends. . . . Then as to the fact of a groin injury, I have inquired into it and it is at most, extremely doubtful. Van Wyck Brooks who questioned everyone who knew James, does not believe it, nor anyone here. There are a variety of rumors, and many obvious lies, but no certainty." Hemingway removed James's name, finally admitting that it was a mistake to put real people in a book. He vowed not to make the same mistake again. That same year, 1926, John Dos Passos criticized Hemingway's use of actual people and names in his writing. Hemingway agreed with Dos Passos. He explained that in *Torrents of Spring* he was satirizing that type of writing, but concluded that it was still a bad thing to do.

When Hemingway began the holograph manuscript of *A Farewell to Arms* in the spring of 1928, he consciously avoided actual names and people wherever he could. He could not altogether eliminate prominent names in an historical novel, but people like King Emmanuel and the Duke of Aosta are mentioned only in passing and are kept well offstage. The central characters were based on real people, but they were not meant to be those people. Hemingway used people he knew as models much as a painter will use a model. Frederic Henry is not Ernest Hemingway at the Italian front, for Frederic is no nineteen-year-old novice. Catherine Barkley may possess some of the physical features of a nurse in Milan but she also resembles several other women Hemingway had known.

Guy Hickok, who read the novel in manuscript, recognized something of Hemingway's second wife, Pauline, in the character of Catherine: "How is Pauline as a blonde? She talks a lot like Catherine as a brunette. Hennaed-up she would be Catherine if you could stretch her up height-wise a few inches."

Scott Fitzgerald, however, was determined to see Ernest doing the same sort of novel he had done in *The Sun Also Rises:* "You are seeing him Frederic in a sophisticated way as now you see yourself then but you're still seeing her as you did in 1917 through a nineteen-year-old's eyes—in consequence unless you make her a bit fatuous occasionally the contrast jars—either the writer is a simple fellow or she is Elenora Duse disguised as a Red Cross nurse. In one moment you expect her to prophesy the second battle of the Marne—as you probably did then."

Apparently Hemingway had discussed the plot of the novel with Fitzgerald before he began writing it, but he did not let the older author criticize the manuscript as he had done with *The Sun Also Rises*. Fitzgerald did not see the war novel until it was in typescript. Yet it is interesting to note that Fitzgerald assumes that Hemingway was in Italy in 1917 and that the experience of the book is largely autobiographical. Although Hemingway did not correct Fitzgerald's assumption, neither did he encourage anyone to read the novel as autobiography. The best part of the novel, he later told Perkins, was invented.

Hemingway's "Resentful Cryptogram"

Judith Fetterley

Perhaps others were struck, as I was, when I first read Erich Segal's *Love Story* by the similarity between it and Ernest Hemingway's *A Farewell to Arms*. Both stories are characterized by a disparity between what is overtly stated and what is covertly expressed. Both ask the reader to believe in the perfection of a love whose substance seems woefully inadequate and whose signature is death. "What can you say about a twenty-five-year-old girl who died," asks Oliver Barrett IV on the opening page of *Love Story*. The answer is, as the question implies, not very much. Because the investment of this love story, like so many others, is not in the life of the beloved but in her death and in the emotional kickback which the hero gets from that death—Oliver Barrett weeping in the arms of his long-estranged but now-reconciled father. What one can't, or won't, say is precisely that which alone would be worth saying—namely, that you loved her because she died, or, conversely, that because you loved her she died. While *A Farewell to Arms* is an infinitely more complex book than *Love Story*, nevertheless its emotional dynamics and its form are similar. In reading it one is continually struck by the disparity between its overt fabric of idealized romance and its underlying vision of the radical limitations of love, between its surface idyll and its subsurface critique. And one is equally struck by its heavy use of the metaphor and motif of disguise. When Sheridan Baker describes *A Farewell to Arms* as a "resentful cryptogram," he is essentially extending this metaphor to the form of the novel itself. That deviousness and indirection are often the companions of hostility is no new observation and feminists have

From *Journal of Popular Culture* 10, no. 1 (Summer 1976). © 1976 by Ray B. Browne.

always known that idealization is a basic strategy for disguising and marketing hatred. If we explore the attitude toward women which is behind *A Farewell to Arms*, we will discover that, despite such ringing phrases as "idyllic union," "their Swiss idyll," "growth to a genuine commitment," it is one of immense hostility, whose full measure can be taken from the fact that Catherine dies and dies because she is a woman.

Let us begin by examining the attitude of the culture which surrounds Frederic and Catherine and which provides the background for their love. In the male world of the Italian front women are seen solely in sexual terms and relegated to a solely sexual role. This attitude is made quite clear through the way in which the Italian doctors treat the British nurses they encounter: "What a lovely girl. . . . Does she understand that? She will make you a fine boy. A fine blonde like she is. . . . What a lovely girl." Of doctors one asks if they are any good at diagnosis and surgery, will they make you a fine leg; of nurses one asks if they are sexually adequate, are they pretty, will they make you a fine boy. Rinaldi's response to Catherine is equally couched in sexual terms. His one question about Catherine when Frederic returns to the front after his hospitalization in Milan is, "I mean is she good to you practically speaking," i.e., does she go down on you, i.e., is she a good whore. Rinaldi's inability to see women in other than sexual terms emerges quite clearly from a remark he makes to Frederic before the latter leaves for Milan:

> Your lovely cool goddess, English goddess. My God what
> would a man do with a woman like that except worship her?
> What else is an Englishwoman good for? . . . I tell you something
> thing about your good women. Your goddesses. There is only
> one difference between taking a girl who has always been good
> and a woman. With a girl it is painful. . . . And you never
> know if the girl will really like it.

The implications behind this pronouncement are clear: if a woman is good only for worship, then she really isn't any good at all because women only exist for one thing and the real definition of a good woman is she who knows what she exists for and does it and lets you know that she likes it. Any woman who wishes to think of herself in other than sexual terms is denying her humanness and trying to be a superhuman, a goddess, for humanness in women is synonymous with being sexual.

The contempt and hostility for women which saturate Rinaldi's paradigm are equally clear in scenes like the one in which the soldiers watch their whores being loaded into a truck for the retreat. "I'd like to be

there when some of those tough babies climb in and try and hop them
. . . I'd like to have a crack at them for nothing. They charge too much
at that house anyway. The government gyps us." Herded like animals,
they are seen by the men as so many pieces of meat whose price on the
market is too damn high for what you get. And the result? Syphillis and
gonorrhea. This attitude toward women has its obvious correlative in an
attitude toward sexuality in general. Coarse, gross, the subject matter
par excellence for jokes whose hostility is hardly worth disguising, sex is
seen as the antithesis of sensitivity, tenderness, idealism, and ultimately
of knowledge. The priest who comes from the cold, white, pure moun-
tainous world of the Abruzzi, where women are safely distanced and men
relate to each other, knows something that Frederic Henry who is down
there on the plain among the whores, who "had gone to no such place
but to the smoke of cafes and nights when the room whirled and you
needed to look at the wall to make it stop," does not know yet and who,
when he learns it, cannot hold on to, and that is that sex is a dangerous
and wasteful commodity and that the best world indeed is that of men
without women. The priest alone is able to carry out the implications of
his culture's attitude toward sex.

The difference between what men deserve in the world which produces these doctors and soldiers and priests and what women deserve can
be seen in the disparity between the treatment of Catherine's death and
the treatment of the deaths of men at war. "'You will not do any such
foolishness,' the doctor said. 'You would not die and leave your husband'"; "'You are not going to die. You must not be silly.'" The tone
here is one appropriate to a parent addressing a recalcitrant child and the
remarks are at once a reprimand and an implicit command which at
some level assumes that Catherine is in control of whether she lives or
dies. Indeed, Catherine herself has internalized the attitude of her doctor.
She presents that *reductio ad absurdum* of the female experience: she feels
guilty for dying and apologizes to the doctor for taking up his valuable
time with her death—"I'm sorry I go on so long." Though the two
major attendants upon her death are male, no shadow of blame or responsibility falls on them. Catherine never questions Henry's responsibility for her situation, for she seems to operate on the tacit assumption
that conception, like contraception, is her doing. And while Frederic is
quick to smell incompetence when it comes to his leg, no doubts are
raised about the doctor who performs the caesarian on Catherine, though
usually the need for such an operation is spotted before the child has
strangled to death. Rather the responsibility for both her death and the

child's is placed on Catherine. In contrast, the soldier who, analogously, hemorrhages to death in the ambulance sling above Frederic Henry does not see himself as stupid, bad, irresponsible. Even more incongruous is the idea of a doctor referring to a dying soldier in such terms. Indeed, when Miss Van Campen tries it on Frederic and accuses him of irresponsibility of self-induced jaundice, the results are quite different from those of the comparable scene between Catherine and her doctor. A soldier's primary responsibility is to himself but a woman is responsible even in the moment of her death to men. As long as there is a man around who needs her, she *ought* not to die. Thus Catherine's death is finally seen as a childish and irresponsible act of abandonment. If we weep during the book at the death of soldiers, we are weeping for the tragic and senseless waste of their lives, we are weeping for them. If we weep at the end of the book, however, it is not for Catherine but for Frederic Henry abandoned in a cold, wet, hostile world. All our tears are ultimately for men because in the world of *A Farewell to Arms* male life is what counts. On first consideration, Frederic Henry seems quite different from the culture of the World War I Italian front. He is sensitive and tender, capable of a personal relationship with a woman that lasts more than fifteen minutes, and of an idealization of love which appears to be the secular analogue of the priest's asexual spirituality. Catherine is a "sacred subject" and Frederic resists Rinaldi's attempt to sexualize everything and to reduce his feeling for Catherine to the genitals. At one point when Catherine is teasing him, she refers to Frederic as "Othello with his occupation gone." One is struck by the allusion because it seems to point out so clearly just how different Frederic is from the culture in which he finds himself. One can not imagine him strangling Catherine in a fit of jealous rage. But when one considers what in fact happens in the book, one is tempted to feel that the difference between Frederic and Othello is essentially superficial and rests only in the degree to which each is able to face his immense egocentrism and the fear and hatred of women which are its correlatives. If one is struck by the violence of the novel's ending, one is also struck by the way in which that violence is distanced to the biological trap of Catherine's womb and to the mythic "they" who break the brave and beautiful. Yet the image of strangulation persists and nags us with the thought that Frederic Henry sees himself in the fetus which emerges from Catherine's womb and that her death is the fulfillment of his own unconscious wish.

Frederic Henry's hostility to women is in some ways quite clear. In the course of the novel, he has a series of encounters with older women in positions of authority. In all of these encounters there is an underlying sense of hostility and while overt expression of this hostility is rare—e.g., the end of the novel when he shoves the two nurses out of the room in order to make his peace with the dead Catherine—it is implicit in the fact that in his mind these women appear as smug, self-righteous, critical, anti-sexual, and sadistic. Consider, for instance, Frederic's interchange with the head nurse at the hospital where Catherine works. In response to his request for Catherine, he is informed that she is on duty and is told, "there's a war on, you know." By implication Frederic is defined as an egocentric, insensitive non-combatant who expects to get his pleasure while other men are dying. This woman speaks from a position of moral superiority which in effect operates to put Frederic Henry down. The hostility between Frederic and this kind of woman, adumbrated in this early encounter, comes out in full force in his relation to Miss Van Campen, the head of the hospital in Milan where he is taken after his injury. Their dislike for each other is immediate and instinctual, as if each realizes in the other a natural enemy. The war metaphor would seem to be as neatly extended to the area of male/female relationships as that of a power struggle when she describes Frederic as "domineering and rude," i.e., not the least bit interested in her authority or her rules. And, in fact, Frederic isn't interested because he thoroughly discredits her authority and pays no attention to her rules. Like the earlier nurse, Miss Van Campen conceives of herself as morally superior to Frederic and is critical of him, implying that he is a selfish egotist, as insensitive to the concerns of others as he is to the larger issue of the war. But we discount Miss Van Campen's criticism because she is presented so unsympathetically and because Frederic suggests that the basis of her hostility towards him is his sexual relation with Catherine. Presumably Miss Van Campen knows that Catherine and Frederic are lovers and is just waiting for a chance to get Frederic for it. She fits the stereotyped category, so comfortable to the male ego, of the frustrated old maid who, because she has never had sex, is jealous of those who do and persecutes them. Her hostility results from powerlessness while his is the product of power; she is hostile because of rejection and he is hostile out of a contempt whose ultimate measure can be taken by the fact that he sees rejection and powerlessness as the source of her hostility.

In the final phase of their struggle, Frederic employs the archetypal method by which men have sought to deny women who refuse to comply with the "feminine mystique" any possibility of power, authority, or credibility. He denies her ability to know anything by calling into question her sexuality and her status as a woman. All he need do to rout her utterly is remind her by implication that she is not a full woman, that she has no sexual experience, that she knows nothing of the pain of the scrotum or the agonies of the womb. So insecure as a person because she has failed to be a woman, the merest mention of the sacred genitalia is enough to vanquish her. In true male fashion, Frederic uses his penis as the ultimate weapon and the ultimate court of appeal.

If the Van Campens of this world get to Frederic because of their pretensions to authority, other women get to him because of their incompetence. For instance, Mrs. Walker. Doing night duty in a just-opened and empty hospital, she is awakened from her sleep to deal with an unexpected patient and proves to be totally unable to handle the situation: "I don't know," "I couldn't put you in just any room," "I can't put on sheets," "I can't read Italian," "I can't do anything without the doctor's orders." Frederic ultimately deals with her incompetence by ignoring her and communicating with the men involved who, in spite of their position as mere porters, are able to get him to a bed. Mrs. Walker is one of a number of weepy women in the novel who appear to have no way of dealing with difficulty other than crying. The attitude towards them is one in which contempt is mingled with patronizing pity. Poor Mrs. Walker, poor Fergy, poor whores, poor virgins. Here, of course, is a classic instance of the double bind: women are pathetic in their inability to handle difficulty but if they presume to positions of authority and, even worse, to execute the authority of these positions, they become unbearably self-righteous and superior. Damned if you do and damned if you don't. But ultimately less damned if you don't, because at least Walker is a Mrs.—no shadow here of not being a real woman—while it is Van Campen who bears the stigma of Miss. For Frederic Henry is finally more comfortable with women who do not threaten his ego by pretending to authority over him. This is part of his attraction to whores: "'Does she [the whore] say she loves him?' . . . 'Yes. If *he* wants her to.' 'Does he say he loves her?' . . . 'He does if *he* wants to'" (italics mine).

While Frederic Henry is willing to evaluate his nurses in terms of skill, one can be quite sure that Frederic would never have fallen in love with Catherine if she were not beautiful. The idyllic quality of such love rests firmly on the precondition that the female partner be a "looker." And Catherine is, she most certainly is beautiful and so she is eminently lovable. While Catherine's beauty is presented as a sufficient cause of Frederic's love, we are, of course, justified in taking a longer look at the basis of his emotion. Although one can explain his sudden falling in love on the basis of the trap metaphor which the novel develops so elaborately—things happen to you and all of a sudden you are in it and there is nothing you can do about it—it hardly seems fortuitous that the experience occurs when he is most in need of the loving service which Nurse Barkley appears so amply to provide. Frederic has, after all, had several weeks of lying flat on his back with a blown-up leg and little else to think about except the absurdity of his position in relation to the war, his isolation, and the essential fragility of life. Such thoughts might make one prone to accept affection and service even if it requires the word "love" to get it. And Frederic, trapped as he is in a cast, in a bed, in a hospital, in a stupid war, seems only too willing to avail himself of Catherine's service. Frederic greatly likes her because she will work at night since it means she is available for his needs not only during the day but during darkness as well. While Frederic sleeps during the day, however, Catherine goes right on working. He is conveniently unaware of her exhaustion in the face of the double duty induced by his continual invitations to "play." It is Catherine's friend, Ferguson, who finally points it out to him and insists that he get her to rest.

The egotistic basis of Frederic's feeling for Catherine is clear from other vantage points as well. For instance, one can consider those few scenes in which Catherine would appear to be making demands on Frederic. During their second meeting, Frederic tries to put the make on Catherine. Because she feels that he is insincere, his gesture simply part of the routine which soldiers go through when they get a nurse on her evening off, she says no, and when that has no effect, she slaps him. Frederic responds to her initial refusal by ignoring it. Then when she slaps him, he gets angry and uses his anger in combination with her guilt to get what he wanted in the first place. Jackson J. Benson describes the situation beautifully:

> In his early encounters with the British nurse Catherine Barkley, Henry is the casual, uniformed boy on the make, but down deep inside he is really a decent sort. In other words, what makes Henry so sinister is his All-American-Boy lack of guile. He demonstrates an attitude and pattern of behavior that any Rotarian would privately endorse. He fully intends (he spells it out quite clearly) to take a girl, who is described in terms of a helpless, trembling Henry James bird, and crush her in his hands very casually as part of the game that every young, virile lad must play. It is a backhanded tribute to Hemingway's

irony here that most readers don't seem to even blanch at the prospect.

But if irony is so mistakable, one may be justified in questioning whether or not it is intended. And why should Hemingway in this instance be separated from the cultural norm of "any Rotarian" so brilliantly embodied in Frederic's anger is justifiable, the legitimate response of a male thwarted in his rightful desires by a maiden unduly coy (vide Catherine's reference to Marvell's "To His Coy Mistress": "it's about a girl who wouldn't live with a man"), whose posture of trembling helplessness is simply a way of disguising what she really wants or at least ought to want.

Richard B. Hovey's analysis of the scene in which Catherine announces her pregnancy is excellent for our purposes:

> From any common-sense and manly point of view, Frederic is failing Catherine in this crisis. When she makes her big announcement and then confesses that she tried to induce a miscarriage, he makes practically no response. The lover-hero at this point reveals a startling lack of awareness, an unpleasing absorption in himself. Thereupon Catherine takes on herself all the blame for "making trouble"—and he allows her to do exactly that! . . . So it is Catherine, the one who must go through childbirth, who does the comforting. A depth of pathos—or of downright absurdity—is reached toward the end of the scene when both lovers concern themselves with whether the pregnancy makes *Frederic* feel trapped.

Later in the novel, in the hotel room which they have taken to spend a last few hours together before Frederic leaves for the front, Catherine has a sudden attack of depression. The idea of taking a room not for the night but for two or three hours, the quality of the hotel, the decor of the room all combine to make her feel like a whore. At the moment when Catherine is experiencing this feeling of alienation, Frederic is standing by the windows whose red plush curtains he has just closed, in a gesture which signals their possession of the room as another "home" and encloses the two of them in an inner world which reflects his sense of their closeness. They are at this moment poles apart in their feelings. Then Frederic catches sight of Catherine in the mirrors which surround the room and discovers that she is unhappy. He is surprised—for how could they be reacting so differently when they two are one and that one is he—and disappointed for this will upset his plans for their last evening together. "You're not a whore," he says, as if simple assertion were sufficient to cancel the complex sources of her sense of degradation. He then proceeds to register his own feelings of disappointment, anger and frustration in unmistakable terms: he reopens the curtains and looks out, suggesting thereby that she has shattered their rapport and broken up their home. Quite literally, Frederic turns his back on Catherine. His meaning is clear; Catherine's unhappiness is something he can respond to only in terms of how it affects him; beyond that, it is her problem and when she gets herself together and is ready to be his "good girl" again, then he will come back. And if she doesn't? "Oh, Hell, I thought, do we have to argue now?" In other words, either she does what he wants or he gets angry. Hostility and love seem very close indeed here and the bulwark which separates them would appear to be Catherine's ability to fulfill the demands of Frederic's ego. Catherine acts as if she knows quite well where Frederic's love is coming from. She is hypersensitive to his ego; she is forever asking him, "What would you like me to do now?"; and she continually responds to their situation in terms of his needs: I'll get rid of Ferguson so that we can go to bed, you must go play with Count Greffi, don't you want a weekend with the boys, I know I'm not much fun now that I'm big.

But there are other aspects of Frederic Henry's character that Catherine seems to respond to, that her character takes its shape from and that form the basis of his love for her. Wyndham Lewis has amply commented on the essential passivity of Hemingway's protagonist and others have concurred with his observations. Among "the multitudinous ranks of *those to whom things happen,*" Frederic Henry lacks "executive will," a sense of responsibility and the capacity to make a commitment. In contrast to Frederic's passivity, one is struck by Catherine's aggressiveness. How, after all, can a heroine be allowed so much activity and still keep her status as an idealized love object? On closer analysis, however, one notices that Catherine's aggressiveness achieves legitimacy because it is always exercized in the service of Frederic's passivity. Whenever Catherine acts she does so in order to save him from responsibility and commitment. It is Catherine who creates the involvement between herself and Frederic; it is she who constructs their initial encounter in such a way as to place them in a "relationship" almost immediately; it is she who shows up at the hospital in Milan so that he can fall in love with her. In addition, Catherine takes full responsibility for their pregnancy and for figuring out where and how she will have their baby and then, when she dies, she takes, in conjunction with certain ill-defined cosmic forces, the responsibility for this, too. It is possible for Frederic to love Catherine because she provides him with the only kind of relationship that he is capable of accepting, one in which he does not have to act, in which he does not have to think about things because she does it for him ("You see, darling, if I marry you I'll be an American and any time we're married under American law the child is legitimate"), and one in which he does not have to assume responsibility and to which he does not have to make a final commitment because both her facile logic to the effect that they are already married and her ultimate death give him a convenient out.

But Catherine relates to Frederic's need to avoid responsibility in an even deeper way. Frederic gets bogged down in the midst of the Italian retreat, thousands of people on a single road not moving, going nowhere and if you try to take a side road your cars get stuck in the mud and you get shot as a deserter. The imagery of the retreat is a perfect analogue for the form of Frederic's thought which turns back upon itself to leave him locked between two impossibilities. He is cut off from the past; he can not get to the Abruzzi, that idealized world of the past where God is not a dirty joke and where social relationships are exquisitely simple. He can not go back because it is clear that the aristocratic and chauvinistic world of the Abruzzi is responsible for the horror of this war, a war of kings and dukes which the peasants disavow and in so doing call into question the whole archaic structure which the Abruzzi represents. But he can not go forward either. His question is not, if you never got back to Milan what happened, but rather, if you *got* back what happened? His mind recoils in fear at the thought of the future. Indeed, he is able to relate to Catherine precisely because and as long as their relationship has neither past (don't worry, you won't have to meet my father), nor future; as long as, like the Italian retreat, it goes nowhere. When it threatens to go forward, it conveniently ends by Catherine's death in childbirth, that "cloud," as John Killinger puts it, "spread by the author as a disguise for pulling off a *deus ex machina* to save his hero from the existential hell of a complicated life." Through Catherine's death, then, Frederic Henry avoids having to face the responsibilities incumbent upon a husband and father. Her death reflects his desire to remain uncommitted and it gives him a marketable explanation for so doing.

To say, however, that Catherine fulfills Frederic's need to avoid responsibility and to remain uncommitted is certainly at some level to say she has failed him. This is the burden of Robert Lewis's commentary on *A Farewell to Arms.* His sense of Catherine's failure is clearly carried in the following remark: "Her death carries the hope with it of the destruction of her destructive love that excludes the world, that in its very denial of self possesses selfishly, that leads nowhere beyond the bed and the dream of a mystical transport of ordinary men and women to a divine state of love through foolish suffering." As the tenor of this sentence suggests, it would seem that Catherine's very adaptability to Frederic's need "to reduce life to its lowest denominator, to make it simple, to make it thoughtless, to destroy consciousness and responsibility in a romantic, orgiastic dream" is in itself a source of hostility toward her. But one can give the emotional screw of the novel one final turn. If Catherine finally fails Frederic, it may be that in so doing she is fulfilling his ultimate need, which is to feel betrayed. Frederic's mentality is saturated with the vision of betrayal. At one point, he jokingly refers to himself as Christ. Like all good jokes, this one reveals as much as it hides. And what it reveals in part is Frederic's instinctive affiliation of himself with one who was betrayed. The metaphor of betrayal also governs Frederic's war experience, for the only killings we ever see are those of Italians by Italians. The metaphor is driven home by the irony of the fact that when Frederic makes his break for the river, he is about to be shot as a traitor. It is the imagery of betrayal which equally governs his view of Catherine's experience, for she is finally betrayed by her own body, whose physical construction is in direct opposition to its biological function and which, in internecine strife, strangles to death her own life within her. It is this concept which permeates Frederic's view of nature (N.B. the larks who are tricked by mirrors into being shot) and which produces his view of the universe in which a "we" who are good and brave and beautiful are opposed by a "they" who wish to break us precisely because we are good and brave and beautiful, so that once again we are betrayed by the nature of life whose ultimate treachery lies in the fact that it makes our selves the agents of our destruction.

Catherine relates to Frederic Henry's vision of betrayal because she too betrays him. She gets him involved with her by offering him a relationship in which there will be no drawbacks, no demands, pressures or responsibilities, only benefits, and then she presents him with the ultimate responsibility of her pregnancy: "I know I've made trouble now." Further, after making him emotionally dependent on her, she abandons him; she dies happily ever after and leaves him alone to face a cold, wet, hostile world. At one point early in the novel when Frederic is going off to see Catherine, he asks Rinaldi to come with him. Rinaldi answers "No . . . I like the simpler pleasures." In Rinaldi's eyes Catherine is clearly a complication and what she has to offer can in no way compensate for the complications that come along with her. Frederic seems to echo Rinaldi's view of love when he says, "God knows I had not wanted to fall in love with her. I had not wanted to fall in love with anyone." And while at this moment he claims that, in spite of his not having wanted this complication in his life, he feels "wonderful," at other times he appears to feel differently. "You always feel trapped biologically," he says to Catherine and the announcement of her pregnancy is followed not only by the rain but by his waking in the night nauseated and jaundiced. The conjunction hardly seems accidental. If in Rinaldi's eyes, women give one syphillis, Catherine, it would seem, makes Frederic sick. Finally, at the end of the novel, we get the sense that Frederic sees himself as abandoned. Frederic feels he is alone in an empty world which no longer has in it for him any source of nourishment or sustenance. And the agency of this betrayal is Catherine, who cuts him off from life as effectively as she strangles her own son inside her. Frederic's attitude, then, is finally not much different from the doctor who reprimands Catherine on her death-bed for being so selfish as to think of dying and leaving her husband.

Let us recapitulate a moment. On the simplest level, Catherine allows Frederic to avoid responsibility and commitment. But in so far as this allows him to avoid growing up, she has failed him and is thus subject to hostility on this account. She is equally subject to hostility for having complicated his life and come so close to thrusting responsibility on him. Like all women who, in the last analysis, let you down, Catherine has betrayed Frederic. We know that Frederic wants to feel betrayed, needs to feel betrayed because the sense of betrayal is his emotional engine and the structure which supports his ego. It allows him at once the indulgence of his egotism in the posture of self-pity and an excuse to avoid future commitments. If Catherine is just one more piece of evidence to validate his sentimental and egocentric philosophy that the world exists for the single purpose of breaking him, then she has once again failed him. *Da capo. Ad nauseam.* The point is that whatever way you look at it, Catherine is bad news. Thus we might finally see her death as the unconscious expression of the cumulative hostilities which Frederic feels towards her. Essentially, she gets what is coming to her.

The use of spatial imagery in *A Farewell to Arms* is, as Carlos Baker has observed, complex. Part of its complexity is relevant to our understanding of the relationship between Frederic and Catherine. Very early in the novel a contrast is established between what I shall call, adapting the terms of Erik Erikson, outer and inner space. Frederic is trying to explain to the priest why he never got to the Abruzzi "where the roads were frozen and hard as iron, where it was clear cold and dry and the snow was dry and powdery and hare-tracks in the snow," but rather had gone to smoke-filled cafes and dark rooms in the night. The tension between these two kinds of space is central to Frederic's imagination. He essentially shies away from images of outer space, investing them with loneliness and fear, and he embraces images of inner space, investing them with an aura of security. The tension is further heightened by the fact that the images of inner space are developed against the background of a cold, dark, wet, hostile outer world. Again, we get some sense of this contrast early in the novel when Frederic moves back and forth between the mountains where the fighting is and where the forest is gone and there are only "stumps and the broken trunks and the ground torn up" and where the remnants of the trees project, isolated against a background of snow; and the town with "trees around the square and the long avenue of trees that led to the square" where he sits looking out the window, drinking and watching the snow falling. This image of Frederic Henry inside, warm, dry, and secure, watching the world outside, isolated by light, struggle against the cold and wet, is endlessly recurrent in the novel. It is this vision of inner space which he seeks equally in Catherine, loving as he does to let her hair fall over him like a tent and focussing incessantly on every room they inhabit and how they make it a "home." When Frederic arrives at the hospital in Milan, it is, significantly, empty. There is nobody in it, no patients, seemingly no staff, no sheets on the bed for anybody to be in, and no room of one's own. By the time he leaves, the hospital has become a home from which he is ejected into the outer world of the war. The height of the creation of inner space with Catherine is, of course, their rooms in the house in the Swiss mountains with the big stove in the corner and the feather bed for the lovely dark nights and the air crisp and cold to define for them the security of being inside, snuggled and warm.

While this archetypal image evokes feelings of warmth and security, it equally evokes feelings of immense vulnerability, for the inner space so carefully and elaborately created is continually threatened by intrusions from the hostile, infinitely larger, outer world; it is but a momentary stay against the confusion of crowded troop trains where you spend the night on the floor with people walking over you and of stalled retreats where, like a sitting duck, you wait to be picked off by planes coming in from Austria; it can at any moment be changed in a moment to simply an analogue for the outside world. The immense vulnerability of inner space is poignantly captured when Frederic and Catherine, on their way to the station for his departure to the front, encounter a soldier and his girl standing, in the mist and cold, tight up against a wet stone buttress, his cape pulled around them both. It is a posture which they consciously or unconsciously imitate a few moments later in sympathetic appreciation of their equal vulnerability. It is pathetic or ironic, or both, that Catherine, driven away in a carriage, her face lighted up in the window, motions Frederic to get back in under the archway and out of the rain.

The threat to inner space comes not only from outside but equally from inside, from its very nature. When Frederic is retreating from retreat and trying to get back to Milan, he hops a train and dives in under the canvas of a flat car where he is out of sight, secure, warm, and dry. In the process he hits his head against something and discovers, on feeling about, that what is sharing this world with him is a gun. This connection of the inner world with death is fully developed through Catherine. Her womb, carrying an embryo secure, warm and nourished, is an obvious analogue for the world which Frederic creates with her. But at the end of the novel we discover that Catherine's womb is, in fact, a chamber of horrors filled with blood and death. In an ironic reversal of expectations, the real danger to Frederic Henry turns out not to be the world of war, the outer world which seems so obviously threatening, but the world of love, the inner world which seems overtly so secure.

The connection between sex and death is incessant in Hemingway's writing. In *A Farewell to Arms* the association is made by the second page of the book: "their rifles were wet and under their capes the two leather cartridge-boxes on the front of the belts, gray leather boxes heavy with the packs of clips of thin, long 6.5 mm. cartridges, bulged forward under the capes so that the men passing on the road, marched as though they were six months gone with child." The idea that pregnancy is death and the womb an agent of destruction could hardly be stated more clearly. Thus the real source of betrayal in the biological trap is not simply biology; it is, specifically, female biology. Women, who promise life, are in reality death and their world of inner space is finally nightmare. Conversely, the outer world of men which seems overtly to be given over to death, is finally the reservoir of hope and possibility. In the handling of these metaphors of space, then, we once again encounter the immense hostility toward women which underlies *A Farewell to Arms*. Perhaps the "they" of Frederic's philosophy can indeed be located in time and space. And perhaps that is why Frederic Henry is afraid of the numbers above two when, in a scene charged with unstated emotion, he stands over Catherine controlling the gas which could so easily, under the guise of easing her pain, kill her. So true to the end is this novel to the forms of disguise, a resentful cryptogram indeed.

The Sense of an Ending in *A Farewell to Arms*

Bernard Oldsey

> *"How much re-writing do you do?"*
> *"It depends. I re-wrote the ending of* A Farewell to Arms, *the last page of it, thirty-nine times before I was satisfied."*
> *"Was there some technical problem there? What was it that had you stumped?"*
> *"Getting the words right."*
>
> From George Plimpton's 1958 *Paris Review* interview with Hemingway

The final act of enclosure in *A Farewell to Arms* consists of less than one page of print, just under two hundred words. In its own way, however, as a dramatic piece of tightly rendered fiction, it proves to be as structurally sound and effective as the evocative "overture" (chap. 1) with which the novel opens. Long admired critically, this conclusion has become one of the most famous segments in American fiction—having been used in college classrooms across the land as a model of compositional compression and as an object lesson in authorial sweat, in what Horace called "the labor of the file." The undocumented story of how hard Hemingway worked to perfect the ending of *A Farewell to Arms* approached the level of academic legend. Some tellers of the tale said he wrote the conclusion fifty times, some as high as ninety; others used the safer method of simply saying Hemingway wrote it, rewrote it, and rerewrote it. Carlos Baker, in his otherwise highly detailed biography, says of the matter only that "Between May 8th and 18th [1929] he rewrote the conclusion several times in the attempt to get it exactly right." In

From *Modern Fiction Studies* 23, no. 4 (Winter 1977–78). © 1977 by the Purdue Research Foundation, West Lafayette, Indiana.

their inventory of the papers available to them at the time, Philip Young and Charles Mann mention only one alternate conclusion separately and a rather small, indeterminate number of others attached to the galleys for the periodical publication of the novel. One of these is the version Baker published, in a collection called *Ernest Hemingway: Critiques of Four Major Novels,* under the heading of "The Original Conclusion of *A Farewell to Arms.*" For reasons that will become clear later, this version should be referred to more precisely as "The Original *Scribner's Magazine* Conclusion," for although it was indeed the first to be set in galleys for that publication, it was preceded in composition by at least one other version in handwritten form, and probably more.

As the papers now indicate, Hemingway deserved to be taken pretty much at his word when he told George Plimpton he had written the conclusion thirty-nine times. Depending upon a number of small variables and upon what one is willing to call an attempt at conclusion, there are between thirty-two and forty-one elements of conclusion in the Hemingway Collection of the John F. Kennedy Library. These appear in typescript and in handwritten form and run from one or two sentences in length to as many as three pages. Some of the short elements show up again in the fuller attempts, helping to produce combination endings that consist of fragments arranged in varying alignments. There is, of course, no guarantee that Hemingway did not write even more variations: some could have been lost, destroyed, forgotten. But those that exist in the Hemingway Collection represent a rich fund of critical information capable of revealing the process of rejection-selection that the author went through to reach "the sense of an ending." Not only can we see in this scattered process the thematic impulses which run through the novel and which the author was tempted to tie off in many of these concluding attempts, but we find in it the figurative seven-eighths of Hemingway's famous "iceberg" that floats beneath the one-eighth surface of the art object. In one sense, most of the concluding attempts that are to be examined here may be considered as artistically subsumed under what finally became *the* ending of *A Farewell to Arms.* Understanding them should lead to a better understanding of it, and the novel as a whole.

All of the conclusions in the Hemingway Collection presuppose Catherine's death. Hemingway chose to present the actual death in understated, summary fashion at the very end of the penultimate section of the last chapter: "It seems she had one hemorrhage after another . . . and it did not take her very long to die." Presumably, that summarization did not take much writing effort. In itself Catherine's death, although beautifully prepared for in the first three quarters of the last chapter, is not one of Hemingway's moments of artistic truth—like the flat cinematic projection of Maera's death in *In Our Time* or the elaborate mythic flight of Harry in "The Snows of Kilimanjaro." It contains none of the asyntactical eloquence of Frederic's near-death, when he feels his soul slip out of his body like a handkerchief from a pocket and then return to corporeal life. This is, after all, Frederic Henry's story, and it is his reaction to Catherine's death that had to be depicted with revelatory force. All of the variant conclusions that Hemingway wrote for the novel are attempts to epitomize Henry's traumatized perception—from which, years later, the story unfolds.

Most of the variant attempts fall into natural clusters that can be referred to as: (1) The *Nada* Ending, (2) The Fitzgerald Ending, (3) The Religious Ending, (4) The Live-Baby Ending, (5) The Morning-After Ending, (6) The Funeral Ending, (7) The Original *Scribner's Magazine* Ending, and (8) *The* Ending (Mrs. Mary Hemingway has allowed the use of some examples of these endings: see Appendix). But a final grouping of (9) Miscellaneous Endings is needed initially to accommodate five brief attempts that have little in common with each other or any of those in the previously mentioned categories.

These five are all single-page holographs, four mere fragments. Two echo material in chapter 1 by mixing rain with the thought of many men and women dying in war time, and they conclude that knowing about the death of many is no consolation to someone mourning the death of a specific person. Another reaches back to Henry's nearly fatal wounding, as he compares the traumatic effect of Catherine's death on him with that produced by the physical wound: in both instances the numbness wears off and only pain remains. Still another of these miscellaneous attempts makes use of the old saying "See Naples and die," concluding bitterly that Naples is a hateful place, a part of that unlucky Peninsula which is Italy. The last, and most interesting, of these attempts briefly entertains the notion of suicide: the narrator realizes he can end his life just as arbitrarily as he writes finis to his narrative, but he decides not to and later is not "sorry" about his decision. Through the first four of these attempts, and a number of others later, we can observe Hemingway trying to find the right linear motif with which to tie off the novel—climatological, psychological, or geographical. With the introduction of suicide in the fifth, however, we are reminded that the end of any novel, not just this, is in a sense a prefigurement of the novelist's death. All of the attempts to conclude a novel mirror the life choices of the creator, and the conclusion of a life can be as arbitrary and/or artistically appropriate as the conclusion of a novel.

"The *Nada* Ending" is represented by three fragmentary attempts to express Henry's sense of being-and-nothingness after Catherine's death. His mind is stunned and produces only a negative response, a form of *nada*. He senses that everything is gone—all their love—and will never be again. But at the bottom of one of these handwritten fragments an added note declares, with some of the ambiguity found at the end of "A Clean, Well-Lighted Place," that "nothing" is lost. The bluntest of the three attempts simply states that there is nothing left to the story and that all the narrator can promise is that we all die. This nihilistic attitude echoes Henry's earlier statement made to a hungry animal nosing around a garbage can: "There isn't anything, dog." And it is this same negative tonality, expressed dramatically, which dominates the ending Hemingway eventually devised for the novel.

Although related to the *nada* group, "The Fitzgerald Ending" deserves separate discussion because of the peculiar editorial circumstances surrounding it. As is now well known, F. Scott Fitzgerald helped Hemingway considerably in choosing the proper opening of *The Sun Also Rises*. What has not been well known is that he also advised Hemingway editorially on a number of matters in *A Farewell to Arms:* Item 77 in the Hemingway Collection consists of nine handwritten pages of Fitzgerald's comments on the typescript of the novel. He so admired one passage in the book that he noted it in the typescript as being "One of the most beautiful pages in all English literature"; and later, in his last note on the novel to Hemingway, he wrote "Why not end the book with that wonderful paragraph on p. 241 [pp. 258–59 in print]. It is the most eloquent in the book and would end it rather gently and well." The passage referred to is that in which Henry, in chapter 34, contemplates how the world "kills the very good and the very gentle and the very brave" and concludes "If you are none of these you can be sure it will kill you too but there will be no special hurry." Hemingway did try to use the passage as an ending, once by itself in holograph and once with other elements in polished typescript. As we know, he rejected both possibilities and kept the passage intact within the novel. In a letter to Hemingway (dated June 1, 1934), defending his own *Tender Is the Night,* Fitzgerald shed much light on his own sense of an ending, as well as Hemingway's and Joseph Conrad's:

The theory back of it I got from Conrad's preface to *The*

Nigger, that the purpose of a work of fiction is to appeal to the lingering after-effects in the reader's mind. . . . The second contribution . . . was your trying to work out some such theory in your troubles with the very end of *A Farewell to Arms.* I remember that your first draft—or at least the first one I saw—gave a sort of old-fashioned Alger book summary . . . and you may remember my suggestion to take a burst of eloquence from anywhere in the book that you could find it and tag off with that; you were against this idea because you felt that the true line of a work of fiction was to take a reader up to a high emotional pitch but then let him down or ease him off. You gave no aesthetic reason for this—nevertheless, you convinced me.

"The Religious Ending" represents one of Hemingway's least negative variants and perhaps the most potentially incongruous. Had any form of this conclusion been retained, *A Farewell to Arms* would have emerged with a much different emphasis in theme—one depending heavily upon a passage (in chapter 3) that has puzzled many readers. This is the place where Henry tries to express the evanescent wisdom of the priest: "He had always known what I did not know and what, when I learned it, I was always able to forget. But I did not know that then, although I learned it later." What is the *it* which Henry learns, and when does he learn it? The usual interpretation stresses *it* as love: the priest's love of God, Frederic's love for Catherine, and the connection between *agape* and *eros.* But Hemingway's experiments with religious conclusions for the novel reveal the *it* of the priest as transcending any mundane love, which can be snuffed out by death. Under these circumstances, the *it* that Henry learns "later" is that everything will be all right if, as these fragments indicate, "you believe in God and love God." No one, the narrator concludes, can take God away from the priest, and thus the priest is happy. With such a conclusion the priest would have emerged as the supreme mentor of this bildungsroman, not Rinaldi, Count Greffi, or even Catherine. However, a question imbedded in two of these religious attempts helps to explain why this kind of conclusion was rejected. Henry wonders how much of what the priest has is simply luck, how much is wisdom—and how do you achieve what the priest has if you are not "born that way?" It is, eventually, a question of deterministic grace.

Another fairly positive ending that Hemingway dropped is one in which Frederic and Catherine's child lives, instead of dying as it does in the novel. Two of these "Live-Baby Endings" were written to be inserted into the penultimate section of the last chapter, to precede Catherine's death. But the third makes it clear that Hemingway attempted to provide an ending in which the fact of birth, of new life, mitigates death. In this version Henry finds it difficult to talk about the boy without feeling bitter toward him, but concludes philosophically that "there is no end except death and birth is the only beginning." Stoic as these words may sound, they, nevertheless, tend to mitigate the deeper gloom produced in the novel by the death of both mother and child. In several senses "The Live-Baby Ending" would have meant another story; and with a touch of editorial wisdom reflecting that of the author, Henry realizes "It is not fair to start a new story at the end of an old one."

The concluding element Hemingway worked on longest and hardest was one built on a delayed reaction, "The Morning-After Ending." In holograph and typescript form, ten variations on this conclusion exist as more or less discrete elements; five are incorporated into combination conclusions, including "The Original *Scribner's Magazine* Ending," as published by Baker, and both the "original" and "first-revised" conclusions, as represented in Michael Reynolds's *Hemingway's First War.* In all of these Frederic returns, after Catherine's death, to the hotel where they had been staying: after some time he falls asleep because he is so tired; waking to a spring morning, he sees the sun shining in through the window and for a moment is unaware of what has happened. The moment of realizing Catherine is gone—something of a dull, truncated epiphany—is rendered in two ways. In most versions, including those published by Baker and Reynolds, Henry merely experiences a delayed response—"then suddenly to realize what had happened." But in other versions his recognition of his predicament is stimulated by a burning light bulb: seeing it still lit in the daylight brings double illumination. Through this simple device, Hemingway placed Frederic Henry among those other protagonists of his who, like children, have trouble with the dark—including the Old Man in "A Clean, Well-Lighted Place," the Lieutenant in "Now I Lay Me," and Nick Adams in "A Way You'll Never Be," who confesses, "I can't sleep without a light of some sort. That's all I have now." His words could stand for Frederic Henry in these versions of the conclusion. He, too, earlier in the novel, gives utterance to nocturnal blues: "I know that the night is not the same as the day: that all things are different . . . the night can be a dreadful time for lonely people once their loneliness has started. But with Catherine there was almost no difference in the night except that it was an even better time."

Without Catherine, all that is left is a light bulb burning in the night, announcing on the morning after that she is dead.

In one instance Hemingway employed "The Morning-After Ending" as a transitional device to achieve "The Funeral Ending." The initial material of this one-page holograph is essentially the same as that described in the Baker version, but this variant does not end with the flat statement of "that is the end of my story." Instead, Hemingway here makes one of his first attempts to conclude with an obverse-iteration method: Henry says that he could tell about his meeting with the undertaker and "the business of burial in a foreign country," but, the implication is, as the sentence trails off, he will not. The same kind of obverse iteration is incorporated into the two other attempts at this funeral conclusion: people die and they have to be buried, but the narrator does not have to tell about the burying, or the resulting sorrow. Henry tells us—somewhat reversing the earlier notion of suicide—that in writing "you have a certain choice that you do not have in life."

It is impossible to state with certainty what the exact order of composition was for all the variant elements of conclusion, since they are undated. But there are good indications that the combining form of "The Original *Scribner's Magazine* Ending" was the penultimate version. For one thing, most of the variations in this group (five of eight) are highly polished typescripts. For another, these versions combine many of the previously mentioned attempts as contributing elements—including the "morning-after" idea, as well as the funeral, suicide, lonely nights, the Fitzgerald suggestion, and the obverse-iteration method of stating-but-not-stating what happened after that particular night in "March nineteen hundred and eighteen." Most significantly, one version of this combining conclusion very nearly became the ultimate one—to the extent of having been set in galleys for the serial publication of the novel.

Hemingway scribbled a note to hold matters on this conclusion, however, and then eventually supplanted it with the dramatic version that we now have. If he had not done so, *A Farewell to Arms* would have ended in the old-fashioned manner of tying up the loose narrative ends in summary fashion. For in the original galley version, Frederic Henry says that he could, if he wanted to, tell his reader many things that had happened since that night when Catherine died. He could tell how Rinaldi was cured of syphilis (answering the question of whether Rinaldi did indeed have the disease); how the priest functioned in Italy under Mussolini (indicating that this is a story being told years after its occurrence); how Simmons became an opera singer; how the loudly heroic Ettore became a Fascist; and how the loyal Piani became a taxi driver in New York. A variant of this conclusion places Piani in Chicago instead of New York and hints that something unpleasant happened to the socialist-deserter Bonello in his home town of Imola. In all of the variants of this combining ending, however, Henry decides he will not tell about all of these people, or about himself, since that time in 1918, because all of that would be another story. This story ends with Catherine's death or, more specifically, with the dawn of his awakening to that fact on the morning after.

Hemingway reached this point in his search for an ending by August 1928. He made some galley adjustments on this combination ending early in June 1929. But he still was not satisfied; the last phase of his search began; and on June 24, 1929, almost ten months after completion of the first full draft of the novel, Hemingway reached "*The* Ending." Tracing through all of the elements of conclusion for *A Farewell to Arms* in the Hemingway Collection is like accompanying the captain of a vessel who has been searching through uncharted waters for a singularly appropriate harbor: then suddenly after all this pragmatic probing there appears the proper terminus to his voyage, and yours, something realized out of a myriad number of possibilities. In less figurative terms, "*The* Ending" emerges suddenly as the product of what Mark Schorer has aptly called "Technique as Discovery."

Even in the very last phase of this process, Hemingway continued to write and rewrite to discover what should be said on the final page of the novel as a result of what had been said in the preceding three hundred and forty pages. Including the ultimate choice, there are extant five holographic variants of "*The* Ending." They are closely related, and they remind us that Hemingway once said the most difficult thing about writing was "getting the words right." With cross-outs, replacements, realignments, these final five efforts demonstrate technique as discovery in the most basic sense of getting the words right, which leads to getting the right message, the right form.

All five are basically alike in form and substance. They are all examples of the dramatic method of showing, rendering, rather than telling. They all contain the descriptive element of the rain, the dramatic action of clearing the hospital room and taking leave of Catherine's corpse, and the narrative reflection that none of it is any good. All include the most important sentence in the actual conclusion: "It was like saying good bye to a statue." But they all state these matters in slightly different ways, using different positions for various phrases and ideas, achieving different emphases and effects. For example, Hemingway moved the sentence about "saying good bye to a statue" around like a piece in a puzzle: in one instance he tried for maximum effect by making it the very last sentence of the novel but evidently thought that too obvious and placed it eventually in its penultimate position, where it is now followed by the line that runs—"After awhile I went out and left the hospital and walked back to the hotel in the rain."

Kenneth Burke reads that last line as a small masterpiece of understatement and meteorological symbolism: "No weeping here," he declares; "Rather stark 'understatement.' Or look again, and do you not find the very heavens are weeping in his behalf?" Burke finds here an echo of Verlaine's line "It rains in my heart as it rains on the town." This critical hunch receives support from the most interesting variant of "*The Ending*," which takes from the heavens a touch of religious consolation. In this version, out of Frederic Henry's reflections, comes a brief line obviously modeled on the Beatitudes: "Blessed are the dead that the rain falls on. . . ." It has poetic lilt and fits in beautifully with the weather imagery throughout the novel, and at first the reader is inclined to think Hemingway made the wrong decision in dropping it from the final ending. But further consideration reveals a sense of craft wisdom. Having previously rejected "The Religious Ending" that features the happiness of the priest, and having depicted the inefficacy of Henry's prayers for the dying Catherine, the author here remained artistically consistent. In eliminating this nub of religious consolation, he obtained the flat, nihilistic, numbing conclusion that the novel now has.

Here again, in this last instance of rejection as in all of the preceding instances, we are reminded that Hemingway's best fiction is the product not only of *what has been put in* but also of *what has been left out*. "Big Two-Hearted River" is perhaps the most obvious example of this propensity in Hemingway's work; it took critics years to fill in the deliberate gaps in that story, by borrowing information from other pieces of Hemingway's fiction, in order to get a full reading of what they sensed was a powerful work of suppressed drama. Hemingway intuitively understood that sublimated words form part of any message as uttered, providing as they do a psychological tension and an emotional context for that utterance. He spoke of trying to achieve "a fourth and even a fifth dimension" in his fiction and formulated a synecdochic theory for the-thing-left-out: "I always try to write on the principle of the iceberg. There is seven-eighths of it underwater for every part that shows. *Anything you know you can eliminate and it only strengthens your iceberg.* It is the part that doesn't show." Examining some forty attempts at conclusion for *A Fare-well to Arms* provides a rare inside view of that theory: it reveals what the author knew, the submerged, suppressed part of the message. More-over, it opens to critical view an auctorial process of exclusion-inclusion, an exercise of willed choice, that closely parallels the life-choices of the protagonist-narrator. Thus we can see that the published conclusion is possessed of an extraordinary tension and literary power because it sub-limates, suppresses, and/or rejects the same things that Frederic Henry does—including religious consolation; hope for the future and the con-tinuance of life (as reflected in "The Live-Baby Ending" and in the sum-mary of characters in the combination endings); the eloquence of courage and beauty (expressed in "The Fitzgerald Ending"); and even the negative solution of suicide (suggested in one of the miscellaneous endings). In this instance, everything that the author and the protagonist knew and eliminated went into strengthening this tip of the iceberg.

Conceived as it was in the spirit of rejection, the conclusion of *A Farewell to Arms* is in and of itself a compressed exemplification of the process of rejection and negation. The only thing that Hemingway re-tained from all the preceding attempts at ending the novel is the core of "The *Nada* Ending." He eventually wrote finis to the story by bringing its materials down to a fine point of "nothingness" and thus left the reader with the same kind of message Frederic Henry gives the hungry dog in the last chapter: "There isn't anything, reader." Within the short space of the one hundred and ninety-seven words that comprise the con-clusion, Hemingway uses *nothing* three times and a series of some thirteen forms of negation, in various phrases like "No. There is nothing to do," "No. . . . There's nothing to say," and simply "No. Thank you." In the process, Frederic Henry rejects the attending physician's explanation of the caesarian operation, his offer of aid, and the nurse's demand that he stay out of Catherine's room. But the most powerful form of rejection occurs in the final paragraph of the book, when Henry says his last farewell to arms: "But after I got them [the nurses] out and shut the door and turned off the light it wasn't any good. It was like saying good-by to a statue." He rejects the corpse; it rejects him. Even in this ultimate scene of nullification Hemingway uses his principle of omission in a subtle manner: he says nothing about Frederic's embracing or kissing the statue-like corpse, although it is a rare reader who does not interpolate some such act. Also, Hemingway does nothing here to remind the reader that with Catherine Lt. Henry had come to accept the night, the dark-ness, and found that with her it was an "even better time" than the day.

But now Henry deliberately turns off the light, as though to test his alliance with Catherine, and finds that the warmth and companionship of love are inoperative, defunct. We can thus understand why, in many of the combination endings, Henry is described as sleeping with the light bulb turned on in the hotel room. Night will never be "a better time" for him again.

II

To estimate the worth of the conclusion Hemingway finally composed for *A Farewell to Arms,* and to get beneath its surface meaning, we should consider some of the literary and philosophical propensities involved in the conclusions of novels in general. E. M. Forster, in his sensible and perceptive *Aspects of the Novel,* makes what may be the most commonly repeated statement on the subject: "If it was not for death and marriage I do not know how the average novelist would conclude." Indeed, Forster believes that endings constitute "the inherent defect of novels," partly because authors simply tire and then force their characters to do and say things to bring about a specious conclusion, or because they behave like Henry James in forcing characters to fit a predetermined plot and conclusion. Forster proves to be an early advocate of what has recently been referred to as "open-end" forms of fiction: he recommends that novelists look not to the drama for complete-seeming endings, but to music and its trailing reverberations as a concluding analogue. "Expansion," he declares: "That is the idea the novelist must cling to. Not completion. Not rounding off but opening out."

Forster was in partial agreement with the nineteenth-century English novelist George Eliot, or Mary Ann Evans. In correspondence, she confided that "Beginnings are always troublesome," but "conclusions are the weak point of most authors." She added, however, that in her estimation, "some of the fault lies in the very nature of a conclusion, *which is at best a negation.*" Frank Kermode, who quotes Eliot's remarks in *The Sense of an Ending,* takes exception to them by declaring: "Ends are ends only when they are not negative but frankly transfigure the events in which they are immanent."

This is an important, carefully worded statement, and *The Sense of an Ending* is an important contribution to the small critical circle of literary eschatology. Limited by thesis, it is an informative and illuminating treatise on literary conclusions as derived from apocalyptic bases. With considerable scholarly and rhetorical force, Kermode traces a line of descent from public apocalypse to private crisis in literary endings and demonstrates that some of our best modern poetry, drama, and fiction partake of this eschatological endgame. The line of descent runs roughly from St. John of Patmos through the Shakespeare who wrote *King Lear* to the Blake who wrote the visions to a host of twentieth-century writers like Yeats, T. S. Eliot, Beckett, Camus, Sartre, and Robbe-Grillet. What these writers have in common, according to Kermode, is a system of literary conclusions that stand as transfiguring revelations. These are Kermode's true endings, which "transfigure the events in which they were immanent." This definition demands a final convolution, the sense of a world ending with either a bang or a whimper, a universal metamorphosis. Although it certainly fits works which are basically apocalyptic, in Kermode's expanded sense, this definition of an ending as something which exists *only* when transfiguration takes place seems if not wilful at least overly stringent.

How do the conclusions of many excellent and well-known novels meet Kermode's concept of a true ending? He points to *Anna Karenina* as a novel with a proper sense of ending, by which he means the epiphanated conversion of Levin to some transcendent concept of man's ability to will goodness. But there are really two "endings" to Tolstoy's novel, just as there are two intercrossing plots; and to discuss Levin's inner transformation without considering Anna Karenina's suicidal *negation* is to miss half the point of the novel, which is based on antithesis rather than simple peripety. *War and Peace,* which Forster selects for its musical aftereffect, ends with no transfiguration in sight: it ends, in fact, with a somewhat dull essay on historical and theological necessity (part of the essayistic material in the novel which Hemingway advised readers to skip).

A brief review of the endings of some famous novels, chosen almost at random (closest to hand on a worthy bookshelf) may throw some light on the problem of concluding and upon the specific accomplishment of Hemingway in *A Farewell to Arms. Tom Jones* ends in marriage and an old-style summary of what happens to "the other persons who have made any considerable figure in this history." *Vanity Fair* ends with a welter of events, death and marriage, a summary of the characters, and a final word from the stage-managing narrator: "Come, children, let us shut up the box and the puppets, for our play is played out." *Madame Bovary* ends with funereal considerations in respect to Emma, followed by Charles's death, the disposition of the child, and the ironic triumph of viciousness, as represented in the last sentence of the book which simply says of M. Homais, "He has just received the cross of honor." After the death of Bazarov, *Fathers and Sons* ends with a summary of characters and a visit to the graveyard, and also with a considerable amount of sentimental consolation: "the flowers . . . tell us, too, of eternal reconciliation and of life without end." *Crime and Punishment* ends with the forced repentance of Raskolnikov in the arms of a reformed prostitute and under the wings of Russian Orthodoxy. Along with the long anticlimactic section of *Huckleberry Finn*, Dostoyevski's must be one of the most suspect and controversial endings in all of literature. (Hemingway, incidentally, showed critical concern about the conclusion of Twain's book, advising readers to stop reading at the place where Huck makes his decision to help Nigger Jim escape slavery.)

These great novels of the eighteenth and nineteenth century are certainly not the works of what Forster calls "the average novelist," but they do support his observation about the dependence upon death and marriage in reaching conclusions. Except in one instance, however, they contain none of the transfiguration which Kermode insists upon for a true ending. His apocalyptic description becomes more meaningful with such twentieth-century novels as Kafka's *The Trial* and Camus's *The Stranger.* Fitzgerald's conclusion of *The Great Gatsby*, with its green light effulgence and pervasive sense of continental ruination, also tends toward the apocalyptic. And in *The Sound and the Fury, The Bear,* and especially *Light in August*, Faulkner approaches transfiguration through the disruption of chronological time and blasts of discordant activity.

But not all modern novels utilize such concluding means. The long interior ramble of Molly Bloom which ends *Ulysses* is difficult to define as transfiguring—except in the sense that all great literary figures transcend the bounds of ordinary beings. There have to be other considerations of what constitutes the proper, the right, the true ending for a work of literature. To begin with, conclusions cannot be made or judged by some outside measure; it is self-evident that they must fit the beginnings and middle of the works which they terminate. Concordance and decorum are as important considerations as claritas. It would be nonsensical, for example, to expect the conclusion of Steinbeck's *Grapes of Wrath* (not to mention one of Dickens's or C. P. Snow's works) to end in some great contortion of events leading to transfiguration. Even though *Grapes of Wrath* contains some of the materials for social apocalypse, its conclusion is true to the naturalistic body of the book and to its sociological sentiment, as Rose of Sharon quite literally provides a starving man with her own milk of human kindness.

Although, then, Kermode provides us with some excellent insights into the literary endgames of works that are essentially tragic in nature, cataclysmic in event, there are other legitimate ends besides these. *The Sense of an Ending* is an admittedly restrictive analysis, and what is needed to balance out Kermode's definition of an ending is some understanding of Martin Heidegger's "zero" (the quintessential "not" or "naught") and of Henry James's geometrical figure, the "circle" of artistic appearance. At the very least, they help account for the conclusion which a young American novelist intuited, through the exercise of his craft, for *A Farewell to Arms*.

It is doubtful that Hemingway read Heidegger's *Existence and Being*. Much more important than any possible influence is the parallel working of minds—the one philosophical, the other artistic—in seeking out answers to the question of nothingness. In *Existence and Being*, Heidegger argues the supremacy of philosophy over natural science, because philosophers can ask the prime metaphysical question that includes "Nothing," or "non-being," while scientists are stuck with the question of "what-is." How, Heidegger asks, can we account for *something* issuing forth from *nothing*? And how are we to relate what-is to nothing? Science simply ducks the question. Classical metaphysicians dealt poorly with the same question, conceiving of "nothing," in Heidegger's words, as "unformed matter which is powerless to form itself into 'being' and cannot therefore present an appearance." Their dictum on the subject was "*ex nihilo nihil fit*"—nothing comes from nothing. But Christian theologists changed that concept by placing God outside the circle of nothingness and having Him create the entire universe from it.

Heidegger believes that we are projected to our fullest moments of truth, toward an understanding of "nothing" and its relation to being, by boredom (which brings us to the abyss of existence), by "the presence of the being—not merely the person—of someone we love," and by a dread that comes to us when "what-is" slips away and we are faced with "nothing." Thus "Dread reveals Nothing." This is what Heidegger means by "*Da-sein*," which he defines in part as "being projected into nothing." It is interesting to compare Heidegger's language in the search for "nothing" and the words of the middle-aged waiter in Hemingway's "A Clean, Well-Lighted Place." Heidegger writes:

Where shall we see Nothing? Where shall we find Nothing? In order to find something must we not know beforehand that it is there? Indeed we must! First and foremost we can only look if we have presupposed the presence of a thing to be looked for. But here the thing we are looking for is Nothing. Is there after all a seeking without pre-supposition, a seeking complemented by a pure finding?

Hemingway writes:

> What did he fear? It was not fear or dread. It was nothing that he knew too well. It was all nothing and a man was nothing too. It was only that and light was all it needed and a certain cleanness and order. Some lived in it and never felt it but he knew it all was nada y pues nada y nada y pues nada. Our nada who art in nada nada be thy name thy kingdom nada thy will be nada in nada as it is in nada. . . . Hail nothing full of nothing, nothing is with thee. He smiled and stood before a bar with a shining steam pressure coffee machine.
> "What's yours?" asked the barman.
> "Nada."
> "Otro loco mas," said the barman and turned away.

Had this particular barman been reading Heidegger he would most certainly have uttered the same words he uses on Hemingway's middle-aged waiter—"Another crazy one." The barman, however, has not been undergoing an experience in *"Da-sein,"* has not been projected into nothingness.

Hemingway, like Heidegger, only in fictive terms, is dealing with the metaphysical question of all times; and the middle-aged waiter recapitulates much of Christian dogma, except that he places God within, rather than outside, the circle of nothingness: "Our nada who art *in* nada. . . ." This parodistic statement may or may not be atheistical, but it is heretical. The principal function of an atheistical universe is to *make itself* out of nothing (cosmologists have not yet solved the problem of how this was done). The principal function of Christian theology is to separate the idea of God from the idea of nothing and illustrate how that deity created the universe out of nothing. The principal function of a literary artist is to imagine and make felt the "nothing" which Heidegger seeks, and then out of that nothing create the something which is his art. The middle-aged waiter in "A Clean, Well-Lighted Place" speaks more for artists than he does waiters when he speaks of the it-ness of being: "It was a nothing that he knew too well. . . . It was only that and light was all it needed and a certain cleanness and order." "Light," indeed. "And

God said, 'Let there be light'; and there was light." All that the literary artist needs to add to that is the idea that in the beginning was the word, and the word is with the writer, whose job is to "get the words right," with a "certain cleanness and order."

A *Farewell to Arms* ends with no apocalyptic bang or whimper, only words that dwindle away to nothing. Lt. Henry is left at the end with much the same nothing sensed by the middle-aged waiter in "A Clean, Well-Lighted Place," by Santiago in *The Old Man and the Sea,* and by the protagonists depicted by Hemingway in a book of short stories entitled, appropriately enough, *Winner Take Nothing.* Henry takes the nothing with which *A Farewell to Arms* ends and out of it performs the artist's task of making his tale, whose conclusion rings with his own words of advice: "There isn't anything, dog." If a cosmic boom-bust cycle is suggested here, so is the ploy of an intricate modernist writer like John Barth, who introduces his *Lost in the Funhouse* with the makings of a Möbius strip whose twisted continuous message reads—"ONCE UPON A TIME THERE WAS A STORY THAT BEGAN ONCE UPON A TIME THERE WAS A STORY THAT BEGAN ONCE. . . ." Hemingway's novel dwindles to the nothingness of Catherine's death and then springs to full life out of the disruptive force of that nothingness and then again dwindles to the point of nothing. . . . The mutual inclusiveness of this kind of cycle parallels Heidegger, who declares: "The old proposition *ex nihilo nihil fit* will then acquire a different meaning, and one appropriate to the problem of Being itself, so as to run: *ex nihilo omne ens qua ens fit:* every being, so far as it is a being, is made out of nothing. Only in the Nothingness of *Da-sein* can what-is-in-totality . . . come to itself."

The true conclusion of *A Farewell to Arms,* the one Hemingway sweated to conceive and perfect, consists of the fourth segment of the last chapter. This short segment is characterized by extraordinary dramatic compression, by a succinct recapitualization of leading motifs, by implicative understatement, by a high percentage of negating phrases, and by the final effect of dwindling away to nothing, with a seeming rupture of chronological time. (It should be said that the first three segments of the last chapter pay full attention to chronological and biological time, using Frederic Henry's three dull meals and Catherine's labor pains as metronomic devices.)

The action of this conclusion makes it as much a playlet as "Today Is Friday." The action begins with the surgeon's explanatory regrets and his offer, which is rejected, to take Henry to his hotel. The second part consists of Henry's forcible entrance into the room containing Catherine's body and his ejection of both nurses: "'You get out,' I said. 'The other one too.'" In the third section he shuts the door, deliberately turns out the light, and makes his unsatisfactory, inexplicit farewell to arms. The final element of action, a kind of one-sentence coda, marks his exit from the hospital and his lonely walk in the rain toward the hotel. To manage all of this activity (in one hundred and ninety-seven words) without seeming to hurry it and mar the presentation, to compress the events in a manner consonant with the inherent emotional tension—these are considerable artistic achievements.

The supreme touch in the conclusion, however, is the provision of a single encapsulating image in the line "It was like saying good-by to a statue." This is an independent creation, based on nothing, which attempts to metaphorize beyond the bounds of knowing, to enclose being and nothingness. As mentioned before, Hemingway shifted that line around in the variants he wrote, trying to find its proper position, and finally deciding on penultimate placement. Out of the very last line of the novel—"After a while I went out and left the hospital and walked back to the hotel in the rain"—Kenneth Burke fashions a renewal reading, in which the rain signifies sorrow and rebirth. "Add to that," Burke says, "the fact that the hero is there returning in the rain to his hotel. Does not such a destination stand for the potentiality of new intimacies?" Although that reading may have merit on its own, it receives no support from the variant conclusions Hemingway wrote.

The image of the statue is more deserving of close attention than the rain in this instance. The truth about death and marriage (and E. M. Forster seems to find little difference between them) as subjects of novelistic conclusion is that, in a sense, all novels end in death. When the book is closed, all of the characters "die," no matter their fictive status. The magical advantage literature has over human life is that we can open the book again and all the characters will pop back into full-blown life. The truth is that all novelists create to murder, and in some instances murder to create. Hemingway reduces Catherine Barkley to the level of a cold piece of stone, but an artistically shaped stone. The Pygmalion myth is here acted out in reverse, and then put right again. For out of that "statue" of the penultimate line of *A Farewell to Arms* springs the entire warm and loving story that constitutes the novel, a story told years after its occurrence. Out of the dread nothingness of Catherine's death, which takes Frederic Henry and the reader to the edge of the abyss, is fashioned "what-is-in-totality" the novel.

The art wisdom implicit in the conclusion of *A Farewell to Arms* is critically revealed in Henry James's statement of the central problem of ending novels, which he made in the preface to *Roderick Hudson:* "He [the writer] is in the perpetual predicament that the continuity of things is the whole matter for him, of comedy and tragedy; that this continuity is never broken, and that, to do anything at all, he has at once intensely to consult and intensely ignore it." As the variant endings here examined indicate, Hemingway struggled mightily with the problem of breaking and yet not breaking continuity in his narrative design. His solution to the problem in *A Farewell to Arms* amounts to a latter-day exemplification of James's astute directive on literary conclusions: "Really, universally, relations stop nowhere, and the exquisite problem of the artist is eternally but to draw, by a geometry of his own, the circle within which they shall happily *appear* to do so."

EXAMPLE ENDINGS

EXAMPLE: "The Religious Ending" from Letter of November 18

You learn a few things as you go along and one of them is never to go back to places. It is a good thing too not to try [and] too much to remember very fine things [too much] because if you do you wear them out and you lose them. (Brackets are used to indicate authorial deletions.) A valuable thing too is never to let anyone know how [how] fine you thought anyone else ever was because they know better and no one was ever that splendid. You see the wisdom of the priest at [our] the mess who has always loved God and so is happy. And no one can take God away from him. But how much is wisdom and how much is luck to be [built] born that way? And what if you are not built that way?

EXAMPLE: "The Live-Baby Ending"

I could tell about the boy. He did not seem of any importance then except as trouble and God knows that I was bitter about him. Anyway he does not belong in this story. He starts a new one [story]. It is not fair to start a new story at the end of an old one but that is the way it happens. There is no end except death and birth is the only beginning.

EXAMPLE: "The Funeral Ending"

After people die you have to bury them but you do not have to write about it. You do not have to write about an undertaker nor the business of burial in a foreign country. Nor do you have to write about that day and the next night nor the day after nor the night after nor all the days after and all the nights after while numbness [becomes] turns to sorrow and sorrow blunts with use. In writing you have a certain choice that you do not have in life.

EXAMPLE: The Original Basis for "The *Scribner's Magazine* Ending"

There are a great many more details, starting with [the] my first meeting with an undertaker and all the business of burial in a foreign country and continuing on with the rest of my life—which has gone on and [will probably] seems likely to go on for a long time. I could tell how Rinaldi [recovered from] was cured of the syphilis and lived to [learn] find that the technique acquired in wartime surgery is [rarely employed] not of much practical use in peace. I could tell how the priest in our mess lived to be a priest in Italy under Fascism. I could tell how Ettore became a Fascist and the part he took in [Fascism] that organization. I could tell [what] the kind of singer whatsis name became. [I could tell how I made a fool of myself by going back to Italy.] I could tell about how Piani [became] got to be a taxi driver in [xxxxx] New York. But they are all parts of [an old story] something that was finished. I [suppose it was finished at the Tagliamento] do not know exactly where but certainly finished. Piani was the least finished but he went to another country. Italy is a country that [a man] every man should love once. I loved it once and lived through it. You ought to love it once. There is less loss of dignity in loving it young or, I suppose, living in it [or at least live in it,] is something like the [utility] need for the classics. I could tell what I have done since March nineteen hundred and eighteen [and] when I walked that night in the rain [alone, and always from then on alone, through the streets of Lausanne] back to the hotel where Catherine and I had lived and went upstairs to our room and undressed and got into bed and slept, finally, because I was so tired—to wake in the morning with the sun shining; [and] then suddenly to realize what [had happened] it was that had happened. I could tell what has happened since then. [The world goes on but only seems to stand still for certain people] but that is the end of the story.

End

[Lots of] Many things have happened. Things happen all the time. [xxxxx] Everything blunts and the world keeps on. You get most of your life back like goods recovered from a fire. It all keeps on as long as your life keeps on and then it keeps on. It never stops. It only stops for you. [A lot] Some of it stops while you are still alive. [A lot] The rest goes on and you go on with it. [You can stop a story anytime. Where you stop it is the end of that] On the other hand you have to stop a story. You stop it at the end of whatever it was you were writing about.

EXAMPLE: Variant of "*The* Ending"

They went out and I shut the door and turned off the light. The window was open and I [could] heard it raining in the courtyard. [It wasn't any good. She was gone. What was there was not her.] After a while I said goodbye and went away. It was like saying goodbye to a statue. But I did not want to go. I looked out the window. It was still raining hard. Blessed are the dead that the rain falls on, I thought. Why was that? I went back. Good-bye, I said. I have to go I think. It wasn't any good. I knew it wasn't any good. I thought if I could get them all out and we could be alone we would still be together. But it wasn't [not like that] any good. It was like saying goodbye to a statue.

Frederic Henry's Escape
and the Pose of Passivity

Scott Donaldson

Sheridan Baker distinguishes between the early Hemingway hero, a passive young man somewhat given to self-pity, and the later, far more active and courageous hero. Nick Adams is a boy things happen to, Robert Jordan a man who makes them happen. This neat classification breaks down, however, when applied to the complicated narrator-protagonist of *A Farewell to Arms*. Frederic Henry consistently depicts himself as a passive victim inundated by the flow of events. "The world" was against him and Catherine. "They" caught the lovers off base—and killed Catherine as one of "the very good and the very gentle and the very brave" who die young. But Frederic, who survives, belongs to another category, and his determinism is hardly convincing. Assign blame though he will to anonymous scapegoats, he is still deeply implicated in the death of his lover.

It is the same in war as in love. At the beginning, Frederic tells us, he simply goes along. An American in Rome when World War I breaks out, he joins the Italian ambulance corps for no particular reason: "There isn't always an explanation for everything." He falls into the drinking and whoring routine of the other officers at Gorizia largely out of inertia. He follows and gives orders as required, but hardly as a consequence of patriotism or dedication to any cause. He suffers a series of disillusionments—his wound, the "war disgust" of his comrades, the overt pacifism of his men, the theatricality and incompetence of the Italian military generally, the final moral chaos of the retreat from Caporetto—which

---

From *Hemingway: A Revaluation*, edited by Donald R. Noble. © 1983 by Whitson Publishing Co.

reach a climax with his plunge into the Taliamento to avoid summary execution.

When he emerges from the river, Frederic is presumably reborn. But is he? Now he is on his own, and he must *act* to escape. Yet he has not sloughed off his old skin, and before completing his flight he will cover himself with that same cloak of passivity he donned when describing his relationship with Catherine—and for much the same reason. Rinaldi was right about Frederic Henry. He is the quintessential "Anglo-Saxon remorse boy," so driven by guilt that he is unwilling—even when telling his story years later—to accept responsibility for his actions. This view, implicit in the text of the novel, gains added authority in those fragments which Hemingway chose to delete before publishing.

II

Consider Frederic's behavior after he escapes the murderous carabinieri—a part of the novel that has received little critical attention. While still being swept along by the swollen waters of the river, he begins to map out a course of action. He considers taking off his boots and clothes but decides against it, since he would be "in a bad position" should he land barefoot. He will need his boots, for he already knows where he is going—to Mestre—and that to get there he will have to hike to the main rail line between Venice and Trieste. Why must he reach Mestre? He does not tell us at once, but it comes out later in conversation with Catherine: because he has an old order of movement authorizing travel from Mestre to Milan, and he needs only alter the date. In Milan, of course, he expects to find Catherine at the hospital.

When he reaches shore safely, Tenente Henry begins "to think out" what he should do next. He wrings out his clothes, and before putting his coat back on cuts off the cloth stars that identify him as an officer. The battle police (who were shooting officers indiscriminately) have taken his pistol, so he conceals his empty holster underneath the coat. Encountering a machine-gun detachment, he limps to masquerade as one of the wounded and is not challenged. He crosses the flat Venetian plain to the rail line and jumps aboard a canvas-covered gondola car, avoiding one guard's notice and "contemptuously" staring down another, who concludes he must have something to do with the train. He clambers inside the car, bumping his head on the guns within. He washes the blood away with rainwater since he will have to get off before the train reaches Mestre and he does "not want to look conspicuous." He is on his way back to his lover, and tries to think of nothing but their reunion and escape: "Probably have to go damned quickly. She would go. I knew she would go. When would we go? That was something to think about. It was getting dark. I lay and thought where we would go. There were many places."

The next day in Milan, Frederic engages in three different conversations that confirm Switzerland as their destination. The first of these occurs when he goes to the wine shop in Milan for early morning coffee and bread. The owner of the wine shop realizes at once that Frederic has deserted: he has seen the lieutenant come "down the wall" from the train and notices the bare spots on the sleeves where the stars have been cut away. But he is sympathetic and offers to put Frederic up, to arrange for false leave papers, and to help him leave the country. Nothing comes of this proposal, for the understandably cautious fugitive keeps insisting that he is in no trouble and needs no assistance.

In an earlier draft, Frederic actually did contract for forged papers. This is the deleted passage, which originally followed the wine shop owner's offer of leave papers midway on page 239 of the text:

> "I have no need for papers. I have papers. As for the stars, they never wear them at the front."
>
> I thought a minute.
>
> "I will be back."
>
> "Only you must tell me now."
>
> "A Tessera [identity card]," I said, "and leave papers."
>
> "Write the name."
>
> "Give me a pencil." I wrote a name on the edge of a newspaper. "Some one will call for them."
>
> "Who?"
>
> "I don't know. He will bring the photograph for the Tessara. You will know me by that."
>
> "All right. That will be one hundred and fifty lire."
>
> "Here is fifty."
>
> "Do not worry Tenente."
>
> "What do you say?"
>
> "I say do not worry."
>
> "I do not worry. I am not in trouble."
>
> "You are not in trouble if you stay with me."
>
> "I must go."
>
> "Come back. Come again."

"I will see you."

"Come at any time."

"Don't forget I am your friend," he said when I went out.

He was a strange enough man.

"Good," I said.

Sheldon Norman Grebstein and Michael S. Reynolds have both observed that when Hemingway cut this passage he tightened the plot of the novel. With an identity card and leave papers, Frederic might have remained in Italy and avoided arrest for some time. Without them, he must leave the country very soon. But the deletion also functions in two other ways: to avoid a lapse in credibility and to flesh out the character of the protagonist. A man on the run, Frederic would be unlikely to repose trust in the first stranger who accosts him after his desertion. Furthermore, to go through the spy-story machinations outlined here—giving "a name" apparently not his own, sending an intermediary to pick up the counterfeit papers, paying but one-third down to encourage delivery, and maintaining despite this damning evidence that he has nothing to worry about—would war against the lieutenant's nature. He already feels guilty, as we shall see. Active participation in illegal intrigue would only exacerbate that guilt.

Leaving the wine shop, Frederic skirts the train station, where there were sure to be military police, and goes to see the porter of the hospital and his wife. They tell him that Miss Barkley has gone to Stresa, on Lake Maggiore, with "the other lady English." After extracting a promise ("It is very important") that they tell no one he has been there, he immediately takes a cab to see Simmons, an American singer trying to break into Italian opera he'd met while recuperating from his wounds. Lieutenant Henry's plan is now taking shape. He has visited Lake Maggiore before—earlier, he and Catherine had planned to vacation at Pallanza, as preferable to Stresa because further from Milan—and surely knows that the lake extends into Switzerland. So upon awakening Simmons, he wastes no time in coming to the point. He's in a jam, he tells the singer, and asks about "the procedure in going to Switzerland." He knows that the Swiss will intern him, but wonders what that means. "Nothing," Simmons reassures him. "It's very simple. You can go anywhere. I think you just have to report or something."

Even with Simmons Frederic is somewhat evasive. It's not yet "definite" that he's fleeing the police. He "think[s]" he's through with the war. But Simmons does not insist on the details, and like the wine shop owner he's more than willing to help. When Frederic asks him to go out and buy civilian clothes for his use, Simmons won't hear of it; take anything of mine, he commands (Frederic probably decided to call on Simmons rather than some other acquaintance because they were of a size). Thus the lieutenant is relieved of the danger of traveling around Italy in an officer's uniform with his stars cut off and his holster empty, without leave papers or proper orders. The way is clear for escape, and before leaving Frederic ascertains the means. Yes, he tells Simmons, he still has his passport.

> "Then get dressed, my dear fellow, and off to old Helvetia."
> "It's not that simple. I have to go to Stresa first."
> "Ideal, my dear fellow. You just row a boat across."

Once in Stresa, Frederic continues to lay the groundwork for his flight. He takes a carriage to the hotel, since it "was better"—less attention-provoking—"to arrive in a carriage" than on foot. He looks up Emilio the barman he used to fish with, lies to him about his civilian clothes ("I'm on leave. Convalescing-leave"), discovers where Catherine and Miss Ferguson are staying, and—most important of all—chats with him about fishing. The next morning, he persuades Emilio to leave the bar and take him out into the lake to troll. They catch no fish, but after two vermouths at the Isola dei Pescatori—the fisherman's island, which was not a tourist attraction like the Isola Bella they row past, and hence a safer stopping place—he learns of Emilio's disaffection with the war (if called, the barman says, he won't go) and admits that he himself had been a fool to enlist. Little else of consequence passes between them, but they have reached a tacit understanding. "Any time you want it," Emilio remarks after padlocking his boat, "I'll give you the key."

Up to this point, Frederic has moved purposefully toward his goal. As a fugitive from military justice, he has repeatedly been forced to act, in both senses of the verb. He has calculated his chances, and calculated well. Finally he has located Catherine and found where he can get a boat to take them to the neutral country down the lake. Yet with his lover he is all wide-eyed innocence and passivity; now he will "act" only in the theatrical sense. He understands precisely what must be done, but waits for her—and then for Emilio—to tell him what that is. By adopting this pose, he appears far less calculating in her eyes. By involving her and the barman, he tries to parcel out shares of his guilt.

After a long night of love-making, Catherine queries Frederic about his status.

"But won't they arrest you if they catch you out of uniform?"

"They'll probably shoot me."

"Then we'll not stay here. We'll get out of the country."

He has, he confesses, "thought something of that," but continues his
charade, waiting for her to drag the scheme out of him.

"What would you do if they came to arrest you?"

"Shoot them."

"You see how silly you are. I won't let you go out of the
hotel until we leave here."

"Where are we going to go?"

But Catherine will not cooperate: "Please don't be that way, darling.
We'll go wherever you say. But please find some place to go right away."
So Frederic reluctantly reveals his plan: "Switzerland is down the lake,
we can go there."

That midnight, as a rainstorm sweeps across Lake Maggiore, Emilio
comes to announce that the military police will arrest Frederic in the
morning, and the lieutenant once again plays the game of "tell me what
to do." When the barman knocks, Frederic takes him into the bathroom
(so as not to waken Catherine, or alert her to his deviousness), and dis-
ingenuously asks, "What's the matter Emilio? Are you in trouble?" No,
it is the Tenente who is in trouble, and this incredible dialogue ensues:

"Why are they going to arrest me?"

"For something about the war."

"Do you know what?"

"No. But I know that they know you were here before as
an officer and now you are here out of uniform. After this
retreat they arrest everybody."

I thought a minute.

"What time do they come to arrest me?"

"In the morning. I don't know the time."

"What do you say to do?"

He put his hat in the washbowl. It was very wet and had
been dripping on the floor.

"If you have nothing to fear an arrest is nothing. But it is
always bad to be arrested—especially now."

"I don't want to be arrested."

"Then go to Switzerland."

"How?"

"In my boat."

"There is a storm," I said.

"The storm is over. It is rough but you will be all right."

"When should we go?"

"Right away. They might come to arrest you early in the morning."

"I thought a minute," is an exact repetition of a phrase used before, when Frederic—in the deleted passage—determined to purchase false leave papers. In both places, it is a sign that he is about to embark on a course of deception. In this case, the deception consists of suggesting to Emilio—in the questions italicized—that the notion of crossing to Switzerland in his boat has never occurred to Lieutenant Henry. This is patently untrue, as the barman, like Hemingway's readers, must realize. But Frederic's purpose is not simply to fool Emilio. He is after bigger game: the raging tooth of conscience within.

III

Lieutenant Henry, in the version of the tale he presents, is provided with every possible reason to bid a farewell to arms. As an officer with a foreign accent separated from his men, he faces almost certain death from the carabinieri unless he runs. But long before that climactic moment, Frederic has brought up example after example of soldiers trying to opt out of the war. Rinaldi, we learn, has few real wounds to treat early in the war, except for self-inflicted wounds. Frederic meets an Italian soldier with a hernia who has slipped his truss, and advises him to bloody his head as well to avoid being sent back to the front lines. The soldier does so, but the ruse does not work. When the lieutenant himself is wounded, the doctor dictates as he works: ". . . with possible fracture of the skull. Incurred in the line of duty. That's what keeps you from being court-martialed for self-inflicted wounds." Later, Miss Van Campen accuses him of contracting jaundice to avoid return to active duty; in denying the charge Frederic admits that both he and Miss Van Campen have seen plenty of self-inflicted wounds. When he eventually rejoins his unit, things have gone so badly that even the Major talks of desertion: "If I was away I do not believe I would come back."

During the retreat Frederic serves as a kind of moral policeman. He not only prevents his men from looting, but goes so far as to shoot one of the two sergeants who hitch a ride with the ambulances but refuse to help when the vehicles mire down in mud. Bonello, who finishes off the wounded man (he's always wanted to kill a sergeant, he says), slips away himself the next day to surrender to the Austrians. In the confusion, Aymo is gunned down by "friendly fire" from Italian bullets. Frederic and the faithful Piani are left to plod along with the rest of the retreating soldiers, who chant "Andiamo a casa" and cast aside their weapons. "They think if they throw away their rifles they can't make them fight," Piani explains, but his lieutenant disapproves. Despite all the precedents he's cited, then, Frederic sticks to his mission and his men up to the moment when he must either escape or be executed.

Furthermore, once he has escaped nearly every civilian he meets either assists him in his flight or reinforces his conviction that the war is senseless and badly managed. The wine shop owner's offer of forged papers is only partly attributable to the profit motive. "Don't forget that I am your friend," he tells Frederic, in the text as well as in the deleted passage. Is he through with the war? Simmons inquires. "Good boy. I always knew you had sense." Emilio the barman has served in Abyssinia and hates war. The wise Count Greffi thinks the war is, really, "stupid." And Catherine, especially, reassures Frederic that he has done the right thing. Yet no amount of reassurance can shake him free of his nagging sense of guilt. Hemingway conveys the persistence of this debilitating emotion in two ways: through Lieutenant Henry's unsuccessful attempts to rationalize his desertion, and through his equally unsuccessful attempts to shut the war out of his consciousness.

On the train to Mestre, Frederic calls up an analogy to justify his flight:

> You were out of it now. You had no more obligation. If they shot floorwalkers after a fire in a department store because they spoke with an accent they had always had, then certainly the floorwalkers would not be expected to return when the store opened again for business. They might seek other employment; if there was any other employment and the police did not get them.

The analogy seems curious until one reflects that Frederic had functioned during the retreat much as a floorwalker functions—to prevent thievery. Then he goes on, in internal monologue, to discuss "the outward forms" of soldiery. He would like to take the uniform off, and he has removed the stars "for convenience," but it was "no point of honor." The abstract word "honor," rising to Frederic's mind at this moment, comes from the conscience which will not let him stop "thinking"—a code word, in this novel, for the functioning of the superego. He wished the Italians "all the luck": some good and brave and calm and sensible men were fighting for their cause. "But it was not my show any more and I wished this bloody train would get to Mestre and I would eat and stop thinking. I would have to stop."

That he cannot stop is shown on the next train ride Hemingway describes, when Frederic is en route from Milan to Stresa in Simmon's civilian clothes. Presumably he should be happy: he is on his way to Catherine. But he misses the feeling of "being held" by his clothes that a uniform has provided, and feels "as sad as the wet Lombardy country" outside the window. He shares the compartment with some aviators:

> They avoided looking at me and were very scornful of a ci-
> vilian my age. I did not feel insulted. In the old days I would
> have insulted them and picked a fight. They got off at Gallarte
> and I was glad to be alone . . . I was damned lonely and was
> glad when the train got to Stresa.

"In the old days"—two days before—Frederic would not have stood for the scornful attitude of the aviators. Now he accepts their view of him as a slacker, a point emphasized in a sentence Hemingway cut from the novel as, undoubtedly, belaboring the obvious. "I did not feel indignant [vs. insulted]," he originally wrote. "I felt they were right."

Ensconced at the bar of the Grand Hôtel & des Isles Borromées, his nerves and stomach soothed by three cool, clean martinis, the same number of sandwiches, and olives, salted almonds, and potato chips, Frederic begins to feel "civilized," by which he means that he "did not think at all." But the barman asks some question that starts the thought processes going again:

> "Don't talk about the war," I said. The war was a long way
> away. Maybe there wasn't any war. There was no war here.
> Then I realized it was over for me. But I did not have the
> feeling that it was really over. I had the feeling of a boy who
> thinks of what is happening at a certain hour at the school-
> house from which he has played truant.

The pattern is the same in the bar as on the train to Mestre. The fugitive insists to himself that he is through, that the war is over for him, that it isn't his show any longer, but then he cannot help touching the wound, striking a note of self-recrimination. Even when pleasantly fuzzy on gin, he is reminded of childhood truancies. Thus he tells Count Greffi like Emilio that he does not want to talk about the war ("About anything else"), but soon brings up the subject himself. "What do you think of the war really?" he asks the ancient nobleman.

Nurse Catherine Barkley provides the best medication—sex—to enable Frederic to forget. That she is later to perform this function is foreshadowed on their second meeting, when Lieutenant Henry initiates this exchange:

> "Let's drop the war."
> "It's very hard. There's no place to drop it."
> "Let's drop it anyway."
> "All right."

He then kisses her, is slapped, and the kiss and the slap succeed: at least "we have gotten away from the war," he observes. But they haven't, nor will they ever, despite the oblivion-inducing therapy she administers. Immediately after telling her that they will go to Switzerland, Frederic seeks and gets her reassurance:

> "I feel like a criminal. I've deserted from the army."
> "Darling, *please* be sensible. It's not deserting from the army. It's only the Italian army."
> I laughed. "You're a fine girl. Let's get back into bed. I feel fine in bed."
> A little while later Catherine said, "You don't feel like a criminal do you?"
> "No," I said. "Not when I'm with you."

But they cannot make love all the time, and when Frederic returns from fishing and finds Catherine gone, he "lay down on the bed and tried to keep from thinking" without success until Catherine came back and "it was all right again." His life, he tells her, used to be full of everything. His job in the army had given purpose to his existence. "Now if you aren't with me I haven't a thing in the world."

Safe in Switzerland, the two lovers ride a carriage to their hotel, where Hemingway introduces an ironic commentary on Frederic's problem. He is still groggy from the long night of rowing, and neglects to tip the soldier who has brought them and their bags to Locarno. "You've forgotten the army," Catherine remarks, and for the moment she's right. But very soon, during the idyllic first days at Montreux, the narcotic begins to wear off: "We slept well and if I woke in the night I knew it was from only one cause," Frederic observes. What was the cause? "The war seemed as far away as the football games of some one else's college. But I knew from the papers that they were still fighting in the mountains because the snow would not come." Later, when Catherine urges him to fall asleep simultaneously with her, he is unable to do so and lies "awake for quite a long time thinking about things." What things? "About Rinaldi and the priest and lots of people I know," he tells Catherine, adding, "But I don't think about them much. I don't want to think about the war. I'm through with it." This is wishful thinking, for Frederic's declaration, "I don't think about them much" is undercut by his next sentence, "I don't want to think about the war."

Hemingway emphasizes Frederic's continuing absorption in the war through repeated references to his newspaper reading. While convalescing in Milan after his operation, the wounded Tenente read all the papers he could get his hands on, including even the Boston papers with their stale news of stateside training camps. After he deserts, however, he tries to repudiate the habit. Riding the train to Stresa, "I had the paper but I did not read it because I did not want to read about the war. I was going to forget the war." Catherine is surprised, the morning after their reunion, to find that Frederic does not want to read the news. He'd always wanted the paper in the hospital. With characteristic understanding, she asks, "Was it so bad you don't want even to read about it?" Not for the moment, but he promises that he'll tell her about what happened if he "ever get[s] it straight" in his head. He never does tell her, yet that very afternoon when she is away he sits in a lounge chair at the bar and reads the bad news in the paper. "The army had not stood at the Tagliamento. They were falling back to the Piave." At the Guttingens' cottage in the mountains, no papers are available, so he catches up on the news when they come down to Montreux. While Catherine is at the hairdresser, he drinks beer and eats pretzels and reads "about disaster"—the war was going badly everywhere—in "the *Corriere della Sera* and the English and American papers from Paris." The night they move to the hotel in Lausanne, he lies in bed drinking a whiskey and soda (liquor like sex makes him feel better temporarily) and reads the papers he has bought at the station. "It was March, 1918, and the German offensive had started in France." During the three weeks they spend at the hotel, his days fall into a routine. In the morning he boxes at the gym, takes a shower, walks along the streets "smelling the spring in the air," stops at a cafe "to sit and watch the people and read the paper and drink a vermouth," and then meets Catherine at the hotel for lunch. During the afternoon of her protracted labor, Frederic kills time reading the paper. Sent out to eat supper, he takes a seat across from an elderly man with an evening paper and, "not thinking at all," reads about "the break through on the British front." When the man, annoyed that Frederic is reading the back of his paper, folds it over, he considers asking the waiter for one of his own but decides against it: "I could not concentrate." He has been unable to forget the war; now Catherine's caesarean has given him something else to shut his mind to. "It was the only thing to do," the doctor assures him when she has hemorrhaged and died. "The operation proved—." But Frederic cuts him short: "I do not want to talk about it."

IV

Eventually Frederic Henry does bring himself to talk about his tragic love affair and about the horror of the war: ergo, A Farewell to Arms. But it is important to remember that we have the story as he tells it to us. Maxwell Perkins, Hemingway's editor at Scribner's, thought like some others that the novel was insufficiently integrated. "The serious flaw in the book," he wrote Owen Wister on May 17, 1929, "is that the two great elements you named—one of which would make it a picture of war, and the other of which would make it a duo of love and passion—do not fully combine. It begins as one thing wholly, and ends up wholly as the other thing." But Perkins and Wister missed the point. The subject of the novel is not love and war, in whatever combination, but Frederic Henry.

Hemingway was careful, in commenting on the novel, to refer to his protagonist as "the invented character," thus distinguishing between author and narrator. And he issued a further warning: that he was not to be held accountable for "the opinions" of his narrators.

Both Frederic Henry and Ernest Hemingway were Americans wounded on the Italian front and both fell in love with nurses. Otherwise, they have not much in common. Frederic is certainly older than his creator, for one thing. Hemingway was only 18 when he came to Italy—not as an officer in any army but as a Red Cross ambulance driver—in the last summer of the war. Frederic, on the other hand, had enlisted in the Italian army three years earlier, and even before that he had been studying architecture in Rome. Unlike the raw youth only a year out of Oak Park high school, he has been around enough to acquire a good deal of knowl-

edge. He knows the geography of Italy very well indeed, as his movements after deserting testify. He even knows how the war should be
fought: as Napoleon would have fought it, by waiting until the Austrians
came down from the mountains and then whipping them.

Despite his background of experience, however, the lieutenant does
not conduct himself bravely or intelligently as a warrior. He is no Othello,
nor even a Hemingway. After Frederic is wounded, Rinaldi tries to get
him the Medaglia d'Argento. Hadn't he done anything heroic? Rinaldi
wants to know. Didn't he carry anyone on his back? No, Frederic replies,
he was "blown up while eating cheese." It hardly matters. He has been
wounded, he is an American, the offensive has been successful, and Rinaldi thinks they can get him the silver. Hemingway was in fact awarded
the silver, but for better reasons. Unlike his narrator, young Hemingway
did carry another soldier on his back while wounded himself. During the
retreat Lieutenant Henry is given his one chance to command, and makes
a botch of it. He orders his three ambulances onto side roads where they
bog down permanently. He shoots the uncooperative sergeant to no particular effect for when the others proceed on foot, the lieutenant leads
good soldier Aymo to a senseless death and Bonello surrenders to save
his skin knowing Frederic will not turn him in. In sum, the Tenente
loses his ambulances and all his men but one, and it is—as he reflects—
largely his own fault.

By showing Frederic's lack of courage and competence, Hemingway
aimed to achieve a certain distance from his narrator. That he was determined to maintain this separation is illustrated by his decision to delete
reflective passages in which the narrator's thoughts too closely resemble
his own. In one of these, Frederic in conversation with the priest asserts
that he loves lots of things: "The night. The Day. Food. Drink. Girls.
Italy. Pictures. Places. Swimming. Portofino. Paris. Spring. Summer.
Fall. Winter. Heat. Cold. Smells. Sleep. Newspapers. Reading." All this,
Frederic remarks, "sounds better in Italian." It also sounds very much
like the vigorously alive Hemingway, in love with all that life had to offer.
So does an excised digression on the subject of fear:

> (When I had first gone to the war it had all been like a picture
> or a story or a dream in which you know you can wake up
> when it gets too bad . . . I had the believe [sic] in physical
> immortality which is given fortunate young men in order that
> they may think about other things and that is withdrawn
> without notice when they need it most. After its withdrawal
> I was not greatly worried because the spells of fear were always

physical, always caused by an imminent danger, and always transitory . . . I suppose the third stage, of being afraid at night, started about at this point.)

Fear and how to combat it was a topic that obsessed Hemingway, but did not much concern his narrator.

In two other eliminated passages, Frederic demonstrates a capacity for love that is missing from the novel. In the first, the protagonist says that he felt a sense of oneness with Catherine the moment she appeared at the hospital in Milan. "We had come together as though we were two pieces of mercury that unite to make one. . . . We were one person." Then, in an attempted revision, Hemingway wrote this dialogue:

> "You sweet," I [Frederic] said. "You were wonderful to get here."
> "It wasn't very hard. It may be hard to stay."
> "Feel our heart," I said.
> "It's the same."

These sentiments are transferred in the novel to Catherine. When Frederic sees her, he says that he is in love with her, that he's crazy about her, that he wants her. But when *she* says, "Feel our hearts beating," he only replies, "I don't care about our hearts. I want you. I'm just mad about you." It is she who insists on their being "one person" throughout. The effect of the change is to transfer sympathy from Frederic to Catherine, since he emphasizes physical satisfaction, while she alone is so romantically smitten as to lose herself in their love. The other excision shows Frederic thinking long and bitter thoughts about loss and the inadequacy of conventional religious consolation. What follows is but part of an extended interior monologue:

> They say the only way you can keep a thing is to lose it and this may be true but I do not admire it. The only thing I know is that if you love anything enough they take it away from you. This may all be done in infinite wisdom but whoever does it is not my friend. I am afraid of god at night but I would have admired him more if he would have stopped the war or never have let it start. Maybe he did stop it but whoever stopped it did not do it prettily. And if it is the Lord that giveth and the Lord that taketh away I do not admire him for taking Catherine away.

Here was the kind of stitchery, linking love and war, that Perkins might have applauded. But Hemingway left it out, probably because its inclusion might have aroused undue empathy with his narrator.

On yet another discarded page of manuscript Hemingway typed a sentence that might stand as a motto for his novel: "The position of the survivor of a great calamity is seldom admirable." Indeed it is not, since no special glamour—rather the reverse—attaches to simply having survived, and when one's friends and lover are not so fortunate, one is liable like Frederic Henry to suffer from excessive guilt.

"There is generally nothing to which we are so sensitive," Karl Jaspers observed in his study of collective guilt in Germany during and after World War II, "as to any hint that we are considered guilty." Such sensitivity finds expression in more than one way, however. Most Germans, Jaspers discovered, reacted aggressively by accusing their accusers. When wall posters went up in German towns during the summer of 1945, with pictures from Belsen and "the crucial statement, You are the guilty! consciences grew uneasy . . . and something rebelled: Who indicts me there? . . . It is only human that the accused, whether justly or unjustly charged, tries to defend himself." But when the accusation is not public but comes from within, the tendency may be, as with Frederic, to internalize the guilt, hug it to one's bosom, and retreat into inactivity.

Actually, Frederic does twice face accusations after his desertion. The first takes the form of the aviators' silent scorn, and he mutely accepts their judgment. The other, more overt accuser is Catherine's friend Miss Ferguson, who lashes out at Frederic in Stresa. What is he doing in mufti? she asks. He's "sneaky," she tells him, "like a snake" for getting Catherine with child and then turning up unexpectedly to take her away. Though Catherine makes a joke of it ("We'll both sneak off"), Frederic is not amused, probably because he is reminded of the dissimulation he has just gone through to avoid capture. So he remains quiet, and since no one else points a finger, he has no one to lash out against. Yet it *is* "only human" to defend oneself, even against one's own accusations. All of *A Farewell to Arms,* from this point of view, may be considered the narrator's *apologia pro vita sua.*

Throughout the book Frederic paints himself as a man more sinned against than sinning, as a passive victim of circumstances. Yet the portrait is not, finally, to the life, as Hemingway shows by daubing in occasional brush strokes of his own. One of these is the analogy between Frederic and (not the guileful snake but) the crafty fox. Walking one evening in the brisk mid-January cold of the mountains above Montreux,

Frederic and Catherine twice see foxes in the woods. This is unusual, for foxes rarely show themselves. And when a fox sleeps, Frederic points out, he wraps his tail around him to keep warm. Then he adds:

> "I always wanted to have a tail like that. Wouldn't it be fun if we had brushes like a fox?"
>
> "It might be very difficult dressing."
>
> "We'd have clothes made, or live in a country where it wouldn't make any difference."
>
> "We live in a country where nothing makes any difference."

This peculiar exchange suggests a good deal about Hemingway's protagonist. Catherine has done all anyone could to protect him: she pulls his cloak around the two of them, makes a tent of her hair, administers the soporific of sex and humor ("It's only the Italian army") to his hyperactive superego, urges him off to "old Helvetia," a neutral country where to her, at least, "nothing makes any difference." But it has not been enough, and Frederic still thinks conspiratorially of disguises and how to keep himself safe and warm. Like the wily fox in the woods, he pretends to an innocence he does not possess; the comparison itself constitutes a *caveat* against accepting as gospel Frederic Henry's presentation of himself. In the end, his pose of passivity cannot hide the guilt underneath, nor can he dissipate the guilt by play-acting or by writing about it. Hemingway's untrustworthy narrator remains a principal agent of both his farewells—to war as to love.

Pseudoautobiography and Personal Metaphor

Millicent Bell

Autobiographic novels are, of course, fictions, constructs of the imagination, even when they seem to incorporate authenticating bits and pieces of personal history. But all fiction is autobiography, no matter how remote from the author's experience the tale seems to be; he leaves his mark, expresses his being, his life, in *any* tale. *A Farewell to Arms* can illustrate both of these statements.

Ernest Hemingway's novel is not the autobiography some readers have thought it. It was not memory but printed source material that supplied the precise details of its descriptions of historic battle scenes on the Italian front in World War I. The novel's love story is no closer to Hemingway's personal reality. He did go to Italy and see action, but not the action he describes; he did fall in love with a nurse, but she was no Catherine Barkley. A large amount of the book fulfills the principle expressed in the deleted coda to "Big Two-Hearted River": "The only writing that was any good was what you made up, what you imagined." Still, there is much that must represent authentic recall in the book. Innumerable small details and a sense of general conditions in battle, the character of the Italian landscape, the Italian soldier, the ambulance corps—all impressed themselves upon Hemingway in 1918 in the Dolomite foothills near Schio as surely as they might have further east around the Tagliamento a year earlier. And there are fetishes of auto-

From *Ernest Hemingway: The Writer in Context,* edited by James Nagel. © 1984 by the Board of Regents of the University of Wisconsin System. University of Wisconsin Press, 1984.

biography, trophies of the personal, chief among these the famous wounding at Fossalta, which Hemingway often recalled.

Why is this last episode reproduced so exactly as it happened—the shell fragments in the legs, the sensation of dying and coming to life, the surgical sequel? In the coda, Nick—who is Hemingway—had "never seen a jockey killed" when he wrote "My Old Man"; "he'd never seen an Indian woman having a baby" like his namesake in "Indian Camp." But Hemingway had been wounded just as Frederic is. The answer may be that it was a trauma obsessively recurring to mind, irrepressibly present in his writing because of its crucial, transforming effect upon his life. Still, in the novel the wounding is not at all transforming, does not provide the occasion for the "separate peace" declared by Nick at a similar moment in chapter 6 of *In Our Time,* often incorrectly thought to be the novel's germ. It does not even cause the novel's hero to suffer from sleeplessness afterward, the consequence of a similar wounding for the narrator of "Now I Lay Me," written only two years before *A Farewell to Arms.* Perhaps in life as in the novel the wounding was simply a very striking experience, the young man's first brush with death. But as an authentic, indelible memory it was deliberate evidence, in any case, that the fiction was *not* all made up. Perhaps, then, the authentic wounding is chiefly a sign, a signature of the author's autobiographic contract with himself.

Hemingway's style, his realist pose, suggests, guilefully, that much more has been borrowed directly from experience than is actually the case. Perhaps the testimonial incorporation of the real, which guarantees autobiographic realism, may also be mimicked. When the "real" is made up to become the "realistic," when the seemingly accidental detail appears to have been stuck into the narrative for no other reason than that it happened, than that it was there, the writer has deliberately made it look as though he is yielding to memory and resisting the tendency of literature to subdue everything to a system of connected significance. In *A Farewell to Arms,* as elsewhere in his writing, Hemingway made the discovery of this secret of realist effect, and his art, which nevertheless presses toward poetic unity by a powerful if covert formalist intent, yet seems continually open to irrelevance also. The result is a peculiar tension requiring the strictest control. Only a manner which conceals implication as severely as Hemingway's can nevertheless suggest those coherences, those rhythmic collocations of mere things, in the manner of imagist poetry, pretend notation of what the witnessing eye might simply have chanced to see. And this restraint is reinforced by deliberate avoidance of the kind of comment that might impose significance or interpretation. It is even further strengthened by the often-noted qualities of Hemingwayan syntax, the simple or compound declaratives lacking subordination, and the vocabulary high in nouns and verbs and low in qualifiers. The frequency of the impersonal passive voice that presents events simply as conditions, as in the many sentences that begin with "There were," suppresses not only the sense of agency but the evaluating presence of the observer. If, despite these effects, there is often poetic meaningfulness it is also true that the poetic is sometimes renounced altogether and the realistic detail maintains its irrelevance, refusing any signification in order to affirm the presence of the actual, whether or not truly remembered, reported, historical.

But this stylistic contest only reflects the struggle of the writer between the impulses to tell it "as it was" and to shape and pattern a story; it is not that struggle itself. The "realistic" style is, in fact, most conspicuous and most successful in the most "invented" parts of the book, the war scenes. It is not so evident in those other scenes where Hemingway draws upon memory—the Milan and Switzerland sections. Hemingway had been a patient in the Red Cross hospital in Milan and had spent convalescent weeks in the city; and he had taken vacation tours in the Alpine lake region. But the action situated in those places in the novel has no authenticity to match that of the great Caporetto chapter in which Frederic participates in events Hemingway had not. Still, it is the war scenes, probably—to turn our paradox about once more—that express Hemingway's deepest feelings by way of metaphor, his sense of the war as an objective correlative of his state of mind. The love affair located in familiar, remembered scenes fails of authenticity though it takes something from the writer's experiences with his nurse, Agnes von Kurowsky, and something from his love for Hadley Richardson, and even Pauline Pfeiffer's caesarian operation; it succeeds less well than the invented war scenes in achieving either the effect of realism or the deeper autobiography of metaphor. It is as the latter that it can, however, be explained.

Any first-person story must imitate the autobiographic situation, but there is particular evidence that Hemingway gave his narrator his own sense of the difficulty of reconciling *Wahrheit* and *Dichtung*. The novelist's struggles to achieve an appropriate ending to his book are visible in the manuscript drafts at the John F. Kennedy Library. They show that his chief problem was that he felt both that a novel needed formal closure and also that life was not "like that." He rejected, in the end, the attempt to pick up dropped threads and bring Rinaldi and the priest back into the narrative from which they had been absent since the end of chapter 26, a little beyond the novel's midpoint. It may be argued that these two *companions de la guerre* are felt even in their absence, that there are no dropped threads, the priest in particular being absorbed into the transformed conception of love which the American lieutenant and the English nurse discover in the later portions of the book. But there is really no such absorption; Frederic and Catherine remain very much what they were at the beginning, this mentor and the skeptical doctor both being left behind. Of the "three people of any importance in this story" to whom Hemingway referred in the rejected opening for chapter 10, only Catherine persists. Hemingway must have decided this made an ending—the tightening isolation of his hero requires the loss of the larger human world—but in one of the discarded drafts he permits Frederic to express the misgivings of his creator. "I could tell how Rinaldi was cured of the syphilis. . . . I could tell how the priest in our mess lived to be a priest in Italy under Fascism," the pseudoautobiographic narrator observes. But he knows that a story must end somewhere. That he realizes that his closure cannot be complete is due to his awareness that life does not have endings.

> Things happen all the time. Everything blunts and the world keeps on. You get most of your life back like goods recovered from a fire. It all keeps on and then it keeps on. It never stops for you. Sometimes it stops when you are still alive. You can stop a story anytime. Where you stop is the end of that story. The rest goes on and you go on with it. On the other hand you have to stop a story. You have to stop at the end of whatever it was you were writing about.

The rejected passage can be read not merely as a device to excuse the odd shape of the novel but as a reflection of Hemingway's personal dilemma, his desire to respect the claim of art and also to get back his own past like "goods recovered from a fire."

Getting back his life by writing fiction was not, in this case, a matter of endings, of plot. The indeterminacy of remembered experience does not matter, because the coherence of events is not so important as the unity of the mind which is the container for them. If Hemingway was to fulfill the autobiographic expectation, the promise made by authentic transcriptions like the Fossalta wounding, it would not be by trying to tell, literally, "the story" of his past. The novelist wrote about himself, and perhaps never so truly as in *A Farewell to Arms*, but he did so by projecting, lyrically, an inner condition. Mood and tone, not events, provide unity, and these were more intensely the concomitants of the present life of the writer than of his younger self. The novel is about neither love nor war; it is about a state of mind, and that state of mind is the author's.

That plot is not dominant in *A Farewell to Arms* has not been properly recognized. Critics who have stressed the prevalence of poetic metaphors in the novel have failed, on the whole, to see that such patterns establish its "spatial" composition, minimize progressive effects. In fact, an unvarying mood, established by the narrative voice, dominates everything it relates, bathes uniformly all the images and levels events which are seen always in one way only. That the principal descriptive elements—river, mountains, dust or mud, and above all, rain—are all present in the opening paragraphs suggests not so much that later scenes are being predicted as that the subsequent pages will disclose nothing that is not already evident in the consciousness that has begun its self-exhibition.

The famous wounding is no turning point in the journey of that consciousness. But even the later "separate peace" in chapter 32 after Frederic's immersion in the Tagliamento is not really a change of direction, a peaking of the plot, though Hemingway's hero does say as he lies on the floor of the flatcar that takes him to Milan, "You were out of it now. You had no more obligation." In chapter 7, even before his wounding, it should be remembered, he has already said, "I would not be killed. Not in this war. It did not have anything to do with me." It is impossible to tell at what point this narrator has acquired his conviction of separateness amounting to alienation from the events which carry him along the stream of time.

By the time he turns away from the war at the Tagliamento in October 1917, Frederic will have had two years in which to acquire the apathy of war weariness. But this is not his malady. Already on the opening page, in 1915, the voice that speaks to us exhibits that attitude psychoanalysts call "blunting of affect," the dryness of soul which underlies its exquisite attentiveness. One has heard of the "relish of sensation" implied in this and other passages of descriptive writing by Hemingway. But "relish" is too positive a word for the studied emotional distance from the perceived world which is in effect here. For the view from Gorizia across the Isonzo, toward the passing troops and the changing weather, this narrator seems hardly to feel anything beyond a minimal "things went very badly." An alienated neutrality governs the reiterated passives, the simple declaratives. "There were big guns. . . . There was fighting. . . . There were mists over the river. . . . There were small gray motor cars." The next year (chapter 2) is the same. "There were many victories. . . . The fighting was in the next mountains. . . . The whole thing was going well. . . . The war was changed." The different character of military events makes for no change in the tone. We are prepared for the personality who emerges into view as he describes his leave. He had not gone to Abruzzi but had spent drunken nights when "you knew that that was all there was," and he had known the "not knowing and not caring in the night, sure that this was all . . . suddenly to care very much," swinging from not caring to caring and back again, from affectlessness to affect and then again to its loss. If there is something that transcends this alternation, the ecstasy of either love or religion, it is so fugitive as to be almost unnameable: "If you have had it you know. . . . He, the priest, had always known what I did not know, what, when I learned it, I was always able to forget."

"Always" is an important word here. There is no hint that Frederic has at any time had a beginning in illusion, that he ever started out like Stephen Crane's Henry Fleming in *The Red Badge of Courage* (something of a model for *A Farewell to Arms*) with a naive belief in exalted meanings. The well-known passage "I was *always* embarrassed by the words sacred, glorious, and sacrifice, and the expression in vain" is not the culmination of a process by which these concepts have withered. His embarrassment goes as far back as he can remember. He has had it always. "Gino was a patriot," Frederic continues, "so he said things that separated us sometimes, but he was also a fine boy and I understand his being a patriot. He was born one." And the opposite attitude, disbelief in such things, may also be inborn. Rinaldi has told Frederic that for him "there are only two things"—drink and sex—and his work. Frederic hopes that he will get other things but the doctor says, "No. We never get anything. We are born with all we have and we never learn." If Frederic may be conceived of as having been also born with all he has, this explains why he is described as having enlisted in the ambulance corps for no reason at all, unlike Hemingway who was swept into the wave of American enthusiasm to aid the Allies. Frederic just happened to be already in Italy when the war broke out. He had been studying architecture. He has never had any belief in the big words. "Why did you do it?" asks Catherine, referring to his enlistment. "I don't know. . . . There isn't always an explanation for everything," he answers.

And yet this sufferer from blunted affect can fall in love. It is one of the "givens" of the story, though it seems to demand a capacity which, like the emotion of patriotism, he was born without. "When I saw her

I was in love with her," he says when Catherine appears again at the hospital. "I had not wanted to fall in love with anyone. But God knows I had." Catherine, as well, had experienced this hardly credible conversion. Although we never get so direct a view of her mental operations—this is Frederic's story, after all—she appears, in the earlier scenes, to be as incapacitated as Hemingway's other English nurse who has lost a fiancé in the war, Brett Ashley. There is more than a hint that she too suffers the dissociation of feeling from sensation that accounts for her unfocused sexuality when Frederic first makes love to her. But now she feels. The raptures of both lovers, however, are curiously suspect.

Frederic has only delusively attached himself to an otherness. Far from the war's inordinate demand upon his responses, he has been converted to feeling in the isolation of his hospital bed, where, like a baby in its bassinet, he is totally passive, tended and comforted by female caretakers, the nurses, and particularly by this one. The image is regressive, and the ministering of Catherine, who looks after all his needs, including sexual, while he lies passive, is more maternal than connubial. The relation that now becomes the center of the novel is, indeed, peculiar enough to make us question it as a representation of adult love. More often noted than Frederic's passivity is the passivity of Catherine in this love affair, a passivity which has irritated readers (particularly female readers) because it seems to be a projection of male fantasies of the ideally submissive partner. It results from her desire to please. She is a sort of inflated rubber woman available at will to the onanistic dreamer. There is, in fact, a masturbatory quality to the love of each. The union of these two is a flight from outer reality and eventually from selfhood, which depends upon a recognition of the other; the selfhood that fails to find its definition in impingement upon the world at large and the establishment of distinction from it eventually proves incapable of recognizing the alien in the beloved and therefore the independent in itself. The otherness that Frederic and Catherine provide for one another is not enough to preserve their integral selves, and while the sounds of exteriority become more and more muffled in the novel, their personalities melt into one another. It is for this reason that Hemingway's novel, far from being the *Romeo and Juliet* he once carelessly called it, is more comparable to *Antony and Cleopatra,* a play which shows that the world is not well lost for love, though nothing, of course, can be further from the masterful images of Shakespeare's adult lovers than Hemingway's pitiful pair.

Affective failure, then, shows itself not merely in the war sections of the novel but in the parts where one would imagine it to have been transcended, the love story of Catherine and Frederic. Catherine constantly reminds her lover of her resolution not to offer him otherness but to collapse her own selfhood into his. She asks what a prostitute does, whether she says whatever the customer wants her to, even "I love you." She will outdo the prostitute: "But I will. I'll say just what you wish and I'll do what you wish and then you will never want any other girls, will you. . . . I want what you want. There isn't any me any more. Just what you want." The idyll of their Milan summer is spent in such games as this: "We tried putting thoughts in the other one's head while we were in different rooms. It seemed to work sometimes but that was probably because we were thinking the same thing anyway." She refuses his offer to marry her, and when he says "I wanted it for you" replies, "there isn't any me. I'm you. Don't make up a separate me."

Their solitariness à deux is only emphasized by their occasional contacts with others who are outside the war, those met in the Milan cafes or at the racetrack who are not the true alienated but the self-serving and parasitic, and even by their encounter with the genuine war hero, Ettore, who is wounded in the foot, like Frederic, and has five medals, and whom they cannot stand. After she becomes pregnant, Catherine says, "There's only us two and in the world there's all the rest of them. If anything comes between us we're gone and then they have us." When the time comes for him to leave for the front, they walk past a couple embracing under a buttress of the cathedral, and she will not agree that they are like themselves. "'Nobody is like us,' Catherine said. She did not mean it happily." Not surprisingly, they both are orphans of a sort. Catherine has a father but "he has gout," she says to Frederic; "You won't ever have to meet him." Frederic has only a stepfather, and, he tells her, "You won't have to meet him." When they are waiting for the birth of their baby in Switzerland, she asks him about his family: "Don't you care anything about them?" He replies, "I did, but we quarrelled so much it wore itself out."

Book 3, the justly praised Caporetto section, returns Frederic to Gorizia where others have spent a different sort of summer. Rinaldi, depressed, overworked, perhaps syphilitic, says, "This is a terrible war, baby," drinks too much, and is impatient of Frederic's acquisition of a "sacred subject." The priest tells him how the terrible summer has made the major gentle. No one any longer believes in victory. But Frederic confesses that he himself believes in neither victory nor defeat. He believes, he says, "in sleep." It is more than a joke, even though in a moment he apologizes that "I said that about sleep meaning nothing." The regressive process, the withdrawal from reality, the surrender of complex personal being, the limitation of relationship to that with an other who is really only a mirror of self approaches more and more the dreamless sleep of apathy, the extremity of ennui. There is a suggestion of the pathologic in the "I was deadly sleepy" with which the chapter ends.

The retreat is reported by a sensibility already asleep, by an emotional apparatus already itself in retreat from the responsibilities of response. "The houses were badly smashed but things were very well organized and there were signboards everywhere." However much this sounds like irony to us, irony is not intended by the speaker, who does not mean more by saying less. His downward adjustment of feeling is the one often made by soldiers—or by concentration camp victims, or long-term prisoners—by which emotions are reduced to the most rudimentary since the others have become insupportable. His battle-weary companions express their own reduction by a preoccupation with food. The entire retreat is a massed legitimization of apathy and a symbol of it.

Frederic's affectlessness is climaxed by his "cold-blooded" shooting of one of the Italian sergeants who has refused to obey his order to move the stalled ambulance. "I shot three times and dropped one," he observes, as though describing the pursuit of game, and Bonello then takes the pistol and "finishes him," as a hunting companion might finish off an animal still quivering where it has fallen. One may say that this is simply war—Sherman's war—and feeling has no place in it. But this does not make it less shocking that the perceiving hero is so matter-of-fact. Even Bonello expresses a motive: he is a socialist, and all his life he has wanted to kill a sergeant, he tells Frederic, who expresses no personal motive at all, and who has never felt that it was his war. Yet for giving up his part in it he has also no special motive. His case is not like that of the demoralized soldiers who are flinging down their arms and shouting that they want to go home. He cannot go home. And now a profoundly significant flash of memory comes to him as he rests in the hay of a barn:

> The hay smelled good and lying in a barn in the hay took away all the years between. We had lain in the hay and talked and shot sparrows with an air-rifle when they perched in the triangle cut high in the wall of the barn. The barn was gone now and one year they had cut the hemlock woods and there were only stumps, dried tree-tops, branches and fireweed where the woods had been. You could not go back.

The "separate peace" was made long ago. Again we must note the reference to a congenital disengagement when he says with what only looks like a newly acquired minimalism, "I was not *made* to think, I was *made* to eat. My God, yes. Eat and drink and sleep with Catherine." Removing his uniform after his escape, he strips himself of the last vestige of social self. He no longer can interest himself in the war news, as he had in the earlier Milan section, and does not give us summaries of military events. "I had a paper but I did not read it because I did not want to read about the war. I was going to forget the war" he says at the beginning of chapter 34. It is now that he says, "I had made a separate peace." "Don't talk about the war," he tells the barman at the hotel. And he reflects, "The war was a long way away. Maybe there wasn't any war. There was no war here. Then I realized it was over for me." But how committed to this war has he ever been?

The rest is a "fugue" in the technical psychiatric sense of a period during which the patient, often suffering loss of memory, begins another life from which all his past has been drained. Thus, the "all for love" that remains for Frederic and Catherine is qualified by the lovers' knowledge that the whole empire of normal being has been surrendered. "Let's not think of anything," says Catherine. The lover boasts that he has no wish to be separate from his beloved: "All other things were unreal." He tells her, "My life used to be full of everything. Now if you aren't with me I haven't a thing in the world." Their universe of two is reducing itself further, and their games continue to suggest this constriction. He might let his hair grow longer, she suggests, and she might cut hers short so that even their sexual difference may be lessened. "Then we'd both be alike. Oh, darling, I want you so much I want to be you too." He says, "We're the same one," and she, "I want us to be all mixed up. . . . I don't live at all when I'm not with you." He replies, "I'm no good when you're not there. I haven't any life at all any more."

These scenes are a drift toward death, which is why the novel must end in death, Catherine's and the baby's, though Hemingway considered allowing the child to survive. Such a survival would have contradicted all that has gone before by introducing a new otherness when its parents are losing the otherness of each other. The two lovers already live on the margin of life. Count Greffi is an even more mythological figure than Mippipopolous in *The Sun Also Rises,* whom he resembles. The very old man, so close to death, is a fit sentinel upon that border they are about to cross before they pass, by a symbolic boat voyage, out of Italy. Their Switzerland is not on the map, notwithstanding the fact that it resembles the Switzerland of Hemingway's vacation tours. In their chalet, wrapped in the cottony blanket of the winter snow, cared for by their good-natured landlord and his wife, whose lives have a reality with which they make no connection, and in contact with no one else, they are united as before in his hospital bed. Their destiny is out of their own hands as they become, quite literally, patients awaiting surgery, playing bedgames. Perhaps Frederic will pass the time by growing a beard. Their loss of connection with human modes of being produces fantasies of an animal identity, like that of the fox they see in the snow who sleeps with his brush wrapped about his face, curled in the regressive fetal position. What would they do if they had tails like the fox? They would have special clothes made, or "live in a country where it wouldn't make any difference" to have a fox's tail. Catherine says, truly, "We live in a country where nothing makes any difference. Isn't it grand how we never see anyone?" The country is, of course, the country of the dead, toward which she is bound.

If indeed "all fiction is autobiography," no special demonstration is required to support the idea that *A Farewell to Arms* expresses the author's inner being, his secret life. Yet there is particular reason to suppose this in the case of this novel which is the presentation of a state of mind, a mood and condition of being. These, it may be arguable, belonged to the writer himself at the time of writing. As a war novel, it is curiously late. In 1929, American society was preoccupied with other things than its memories of the battles of the First World War. Hemingway, already the author of a novel dealing with a later period and married for the second time, had come a long way from the naive nineteen-year-old of 1918. Any such analysis is speculative, but there is reason to suppose that for the writer as for Frederic Henry the barn was gone where he had lain in the hay as a boy: "You could not go back." This realization must have been particularly acute when this novel was being written. Since 1925 his life had been one of personal turmoil. He had found himself in love with Pauline Pfeiffer, forced to decide between her and the woman whom he still claimed also to love and who had been, he would declare, a faultless wife. In 1927, he had remarried and, in the following year, while Pauline was pregnant, he was struggling to make progress on this second novel, plagued by various accidental disasters—an eye injury, head cuts from a fallen skylight—such as he always seemed prone to. Pauline's baby was delivered by caesarian section after a labor of eighteen hours during a Kansas heat wave. The first draft of *A Farewell to Arms* was finished two months later, but before Hemingway began the task of revision, his father, Dr. Clarence Hemingway, who had been depressed for some time, committed suicide by shooting himself in the head.

Beyond the immediate strain and horror of such events must have been their power to intensify Hemingway's most buried anxieties. His remarriage, which he did not quite understand, created a keen sense of guilt in him along with the recognition that he contained compulsive forces he was powerless to restrain. Marriage, moreover, could be destructive not only because it had resulted in pain and divorce in his own case; as a child he had seen its effects in the secret contests of will between his parents. Pauline's dangerous, agonized parturition seemed to confirm his feeling that death as readily as life was the consequence of sexuality. He may well have felt what he had imagined the Indian father to feel before cutting his throat in "Indian Camp." That early story suggests that Hemingway had always seen something terrifying in the birth process. Now he incorporated a birth process fatal to both fictional mother and child in the conclusion of his novel.

His father's suicide must have awakened further all his most inadmissible emotions, above all his feelings of hostility and guilt toward his parents. Readers of Carlos Baker's biography do not need a review of Hemingway's childhood and youth with its history of rebellions and chastisements. The spirited boy, adoring and striving to emulate his father, also incurred this father's disciplinarian severity, and young Ernest's resentment of his punishment was so intense that he would sometimes, when he was about eighteen, sit hidden in the doorway of a shed behind the house drawing a bead on his father's head with a gun while the doctor worked in his vegetable garden. Yet it was this same father who had taught him to shoot, initiated him in the craft and passion of killing animals. His feelings toward his mother, whose musical-artistic inclinations might be thought to be the source of his own impulses toward the life of art, would, in the end, prove more bitterly hostile. As he grew to manhood he felt, it would seem, more betrayed by her attempts to control his behavior, especially after the war had proved him a man and even a hero. There is the well-known incident of youthful high-jinks in the woods, shortly after his twenty-first birthday, which resulted in his expulsion from the Hemingways' summer cottage at Walloon Lake. But more hurtful must have been his parents' moralistic censure of his writing. First *In Our Time* and then *The Sun Also Rises* received their uncomprehending disapproval, against which he politely pleaded.

Beneath the politeness there was sometimes a threat. After receiving her criticism of his first novel Hemingway wrote his mother with only half-concealed scorn, "I am sure that it [the novel] is not more unpleasant than the real inner lives of some of our best Oak Park families. You must remember that in such a book all the worst of the people's lives is displayed while at home there is a very lovely side for the public and the sort of which I have had some experience of observing behind closed doors." Behind what doors but those closed upon the conflicts he had known between his parents themselves? Hemingway was prone to hint for years that he might write an Oak Park novel that would tell all: "I had a wonderful novel to write about Oak Park," he said in 1952, "and would never do it because I did not want to hurt living people." After his father's death in 1928 he wrote his mother offering her some advice about how to handle his uncle George, whom he held responsible for his father's money worries, and he also added menacingly, "I have never written a novel about the [Hemingway] family because I have never wanted to hurt anyone's feelings but with the death of the ones I love a period has been put to a great part of it and I may have to undertake it." It is a curious statement, with its slip into the plural "ones" when among his near relatives only his father had died. And was not his mother to be counted among the "ones I love?" There seems to be an unclear implication that she as much as his uncle—whom he had always disliked—might be exposed by his writing. The Oak Park novel was never written. Yet if he rejected the temptation to write about his family life—except in the hints given in such a story as "The Doctor and the Doctor's Wife"—he did not stop writing works that might convey his insight into the "unpleasant" and defy his mother's moralistic hypocrisy. And the covertly autobiographic impulse persisted.

From the time of his father's suicide, he must have felt himself to be just such an orphan, though with a living parent, as Catherine and Frederic describe themselves. "My father is the only one I cared about," he wrote Maxwell Perkins after the doctor's suicide. He then may already have believed what he later stated to Charles Scribner, that his mother had destroyed her husband, and his bitter sense of having been unloved by her fused with his identification with his father: "I hate her guts and she hates mine. She forced my father to suicide." But such liberations from filial love are never quite complete. Underneath must have been the longing for approval, for a lost infantile security. Hemingway's own sexual history, that ultimate personal expression, may have taken some shape from the mixture of need and anger which probably composed his emotions toward his mother. The need to reject as well as the need to be wanted again may explain the course of his love life, with its four marriages and, as his life advanced, its rather greater propensity of promiscuity. Promiscuity, of course, may also be based on the fear that one cannot feel at all. Beneath the intensely expressive, even violent personality of the visible Hemingway there may have been a self that was haunted by the demon of boredom. Apathy, which might seem the least likely affliction of this articulate and active man, may have been what he feared most, knowing his own inner indifference. If so, then *A Farewell to Arms* does have a special relation to the mind of the maker, is autobiographic in a metaphoric way.

Some confirmation of this view may be gained by study of Hemingway's text as the result of revision and excision in accordance with his well-known iceberg theory. In looking for the submerged element that supports a style so economic, so dependent upon implication rather than explication, one is prompted to consider the nature of what has been pruned away. Obviously, the Hemingway aesthetic promotes the elimination of the merely redundant, the detail that adds nothing, the explanation that can be supplied by the reader's own surmise, the additional episode which may thicken the reality of the story but also complicates its meaning too much. Some of this discard may well supply autobiographic clues to the intentional process by which the work was molded. Sometimes, one suspects, the rejected matter comes out of the too-exact transcript of memory.

Even before the manuscript of *A Farewell to Arms* had been studied, it was obvious that Hemingway might have planned his novel at some earlier stage to include other elements besides those finally selected. Julian Smith has argued that two stories written in 1926 just after the breakup of Hemingway's first marriage amplify the novel so precisely at certain points that they may have been conceived of as part of it at one time. One of these is "In Another Country," whose title, with its reference to Marlowe's *Jew of Malta* ("Thou hast committed— / Fornication—but that was in another country; and besides, the wench is dead"), Hemingway once considered using for the novel. The second story linked with the novel is "Now I Lay Me," entitled "In Another Country—Two" in a late draft. Both short stories fulfill the title of the collection in which they were printed in 1927, *Men without Women,* which attaches them in an interesting way to the novel begun soon after, the novel about the failure, in the end, of the sexual bridge over the gulf of solitude.

Both stories are really about marriage. In "In Another Country" the narrator, recovering from his wounds in a Milan hospital and receiving mechanical therapy—like Hemingway and Frederic Henry—is warned not to marry. An Italian major who has just lost his wife tells him that a man "cannot marry" because "if he is to lose everything, he should not place himself in a position to lose that." Had Hemingway chosen to include the story as an episode in *A Farewell to Arms* it might have served to predict Catherine's death as well as the conclusion that nothing, not even love, abides. In "Now I Lay Me" the hero has been wounded in the particular fashion and with the particular sensations Hemingway remembered from his own experience and attributed to Frederic. He does not sleep well—because of the sound of the silkworms and because he is afraid of dying—and passes restless nights thinking about two kinds of boyhood experience: trout fishing and the quarrels between his parents, with his mother's hen-pecking of his father. He is advised by his orderly *to* marry but does not, and does not intend to, unlike the narrator of the companion story, who tells the major that he hopes to be married.

There are any number of ways in which both stories can be related to Hemingway's personal experience, but it is clear that together they suggest a fear associated with marriage—either one will somehow kill it oneself, as he had done with his own first marriage, or it will kill you, or at least emasculate you, as his mother had emasculated his father. Despite the seemingly positive assurance of the orderly in the second story that marriage will "fix everything," the effect of both tales is to suggest that death and destruction arrive in the end. Love cannot heal the Hemingway hero who longs to return to some presexual condition in the untainted woods of boyhood.

The connection of the two stories with the novel written so soon after them is a matter of conjecture, but Hemingway's manuscript drafts of *A Farewell to Arms* may justifiably be searched for evidence of his compositional intentions and his autobiographic sources. The draft indicates that Hemingway had, for example, included a much more detailed version of the description of wounding already used in "Now I Lay Me" and also a more detailed and more emotional description of Frederic's sensations on waking up in the hospital in Milan. The final version screens out autobiographic irrelevance, for Frederic, in the draft, makes on Hemingway's behalf one of those representative comments that show him struggling against the flood of memory: "If you try and put in everything you would never get a single day done and then the one who made it might not feel it." In the end the writer made these occasions consistent with the rest of the novel as a representation of the state of mind that is the grounding of his hero's being. In the first three books, as Reynolds has observed, the revisions nearly efface Frederic as a personality. He becomes an almost completely apathetic sufferer. Though self-expression is allowed to emerge in the love affair, it does not really make for reversal of this condition, for in the place of the grand afflatus of love, the language of amorous avowal that these lovers speak is self-diminishing.

A complex revision of a crucial passage is the alteration of the conversation between Frederic and the priest in chapter 11. In the manuscript draft Frederic lists some of the things he loves, and adds at the end, "I found I loved god too, a little. I did not love anything too much." In the revision there is no such list or remark, but there is, instead, the priest's statement: "When you love you wish to do things for. You wish to sacrifice for. You wish to serve." Hemingway may be thought to have promoted by this addition the hope of moral growth in his hero, who then asks, in the printed text, "How about loving a woman? If I really loved some woman would it be like that?" He cannot answer his own question nor does the priest answer it, and though, much later, Count Greffi calls love "a religious feeling," Frederic, still dubious, can respond only, "You think so?" Can we analogize the love of God and Frederic's love of Catherine, in fact? Does human love acquire the highest possible meaning for him? Not really. He cannot be said to attain the priest's ideal of service and sacrifice. Nor does the formula apply to Catherine herself. Her death is not redemptive, is not a true Imitation of Christ. It is not voluntarily offered and does not save Frederic from anything or give him faith. Only irony attends the sequel in which the surrender of self seems the consequence of weakness rather than the bounty of strong love. The revision removes the small assertion of faith that Frederic makes, "I found I loved god too, a little," and when the priest declares, "You should love Him," the answer is simply, "I don't love much," or, as the draft has it, "I did not love anything very much," which seems a statement of affective deficiency in general, a general inability to donate emotion.

Frederic's estrangement from feeling is not the consequence of any particular wounding or of war disgust, or of any experience of adulthood, but of a deeply founded sense of loss. A passage Hemingway took out of the novel gives confirmation. It begins with the opening sentence of chapter 40, "We had a fine life," followed in the finished novel by a brief description of the way the couple spent their days during the last of their winter stay in the Swiss mountains. Hemingway decided not to use the long passage that originally followed this opening sentence in which Frederic reflects, anticipating the tragic conclusion, "wisdom and happiness do not go together," and declares his reductive certitude: "The only thing

I know is that if you love anything enough they take it away from you."
In this discarded passage, as in the rejected ending of the novel, Hemingway felt the need to refer once again to Rinaldi and the priest, those seemingly forgotten mentors of contrary wisdom, and it is plain that Frederic cannot accept the latter's faith, though he says, "I see the wisdom of the priest in our mess who has always loved God and so is happy and I am sure that nothing will ever take God away from him. But how much is wisdom and how much is luck to be born that way? And what if you are not built that way?" Earlier in the novel Gino is described as a patriot because he is "born that way" and Rinaldi is a skeptic for the same reason. But here, in the excised passage, Frederic speaks of himself: "But what if you were born loving nothing and the warm milk of your mother's breast was never heaven and the first thing you loved was the side of a hill and the last thing was a woman and they took her away and you did not want another but only to have her; and she was gone, then you are not so well placed." For Hemingway, too, cannot it have been true that "the warm milk of [his] mother's breast was never heaven?" Is this the underwater knowledge of self which supports the poignancy of what remains in the final text of the novel?

Hemingway's difficulties with the ending can now be seen to have been caused by something besides his desire to be true to life's inconclusiveness. His hero's emotional or philosophic *nada* threatened the very process of making sense, achieving illumination. Hemingway decided to eschew any hint of apocalypse, rejecting even Fitzgerald's suggestion that he place at the end the passage in which Frederic describes how all are finished off impartially, though the good, the gentle, and the brave go first—as dark a revelation as one could imagine, but still a revelation of sorts. What would do best, he realized, would be simply the hero's numb survival without insight, his notation without catharsis.

Catherine Barkley and the Hemingway Code: Ritual and Survival in *A Farewell to Arms*

Sandra Whipple Spanier

> *"If men could see us as we really are, they would be a little amazed; but the cleverest, the acutest men are often under an illusion about women: they do not read them in a true light: they misapprehend them, both for good and for evil: their good woman is a queer thing, half doll, half angel; their bad woman almost always a fiend."*
>
> CHARLOTTE BRONTË, *Shirley*

It is a critical commonplace that there are two kinds of Hemingway women: the destructive ones and the daydreams. Catherine Barkley long has been regarded as the ultimate dreamgirl: "a divine lollipop," in the words of Frances Hackett; "the abstraction of a lyric emotion," according to Edmund Wilson; "idealized past the fondest belief of most people and even the more realistic wishes of some," says Philip Young. To others the dream is a nightmare. Devoid of any personality or character of her own, Catherine becomes Frederic Henry's "leechlike shadow," the siren luring the young man to his destruction through her isolating love (Leo Gurko). Most feminist critics also have assumed Catherine as the antithesis of Frederic, whether objecting to her voluntary submissiveness or simply dismissing her as a colorless figment of the male imagination. Millicent Bell calls her "a sort of inflated rubber doll woman available at will to the onanistic dreamer," and Judith Fetterley views her idealization as a mask for both Frederic's fear of Catherine and his hostility toward her—the message of her death that "the only good woman is a dead one."

Recently some critics have begun to recognize an overlooked sympathy and respect for women in Hemingway's work. Linda Wagner, for example, argues persuasively that in much of Hemingway's early fiction, "the women have already reached that plateau of semi-stoic self-awareness which Hemingway's men have, usually, yet to attain"—but she specifically excludes Catherine Barkley, citing her "submissiveness and languor." Only Joyce Wexler has made a full-fledged argument for Catherine's strength of character, as a woman "neither demeaned nor idealized by Hemingway," but rather presented as a forerunner of the kind of person Frederic has become by the time he narrates the story.

Wexler breaks new ground when she declares that Frederic and Catherine are "members of the same species, Hemingway heroes," but I would quibble with her terminology. In the terms that have become almost standard vocabulary for talking about the recurring pattern of characterization in Hemingway's fiction, Frederic Henry alone is a "Hemingway hero." Catherine Barkley not only is a strong and fully realized character, she is the one character in this novel who exemplifies in the widest range the controls of honor and courage, the "grace under pressure" that have come to be known as the "Hemingway code." Her part is to teach Frederic Henry by example how to survive in a hostile and chaotic world in which an individual can gain at most a limited autonomy—through scrupulous adherence to roles and rituals of one's own devising. She is the code hero of this novel if anyone is.

Such a reading must rest on the evidence of the text, and I hope to show that it does. But beyond that, this study will explore *why* Catherine Barkley has been so consistently overlooked as the exemplar of this novel, and it will examine the ways in which other, external sources of reference—the posthumously published *Garden of Eden* and especially the unpublished manuscripts of *A Farewell to Arms*—further support the view that Catherine Barkley is the one in control, in the best tradition of the Hemingway code.

I

In the list of possible titles that Hemingway wisely rejected for his novel (including "Love in Italy," "Death Once Dead," and "They Who Get Shot") is "The Sentimental Education of Frederic Henry." *A Farewell to Arms* is a novel of education, following the pattern of much of Hemingway's fiction, in which a young man raised in the American Middle West confronts the senseless horrors of modern existence and must learn to devise a means to survive keeping the greatest possible portion of his sanity and dignity intact. This young man, sharing many experiences of the author, has come to be known as the "Hemingway hero," and playing opposite him in many works is another character, the "code hero"—that person already initiated into the cruelties and absurdities of life, who has devised practical means to cope, a way to live "holding tight."

Frederic Henry is the classic Hemingway hero, but a code hero in *A Farewell to Arms* is not so easy to find. Several of the minor characters exemplify aspects of the Hemingway code: Dr. Valentini, the competent and good-humored surgeon who decides to operate immediately on Frederic's knee; the ancient and worldly Count Greffi; and the British major who declared, "We were all cooked. The thing was not to realize it."

More fully developed as possible mentors for Frederic are the priest and Rinaldi, the man of faith and the self-proclaimed "snake of reason," who represent alternate—really dichotomous—visions for coping with experience. At the front he shares a special bond with each. Frederic alone takes no part in the hilarity of "priest baiting," and he regrets that he had not spent his leave with the priest's family in the Abruzzi, where it was "clear cold and dry . . . and the peasants took off their hats and called you Lord." Yet in his cynicism and devotion to sensory pleasures, Frederic shares a special bond with Rinaldi, too, and Rinaldi claims him as kin: "With your priest and your English girl, and really you are just like me underneath. . . . You are really an Italian. All fire and smoke and nothing inside."

But when Frederic returns from his convalescence in Milan, where he had fallen in love with Catherine, he finds the priest weary and depressed. Rinaldi is exhausted, probably syphilitic, and has come to the bitter recognition that besides his work he likes only two other things: "One is bad for my work and the other is over in half an hour or fifteen minutes. Sometimes less." Rinaldi's cynicism is fundamentally bankrupt, and the priest's faithful orthodoxy impotent to counter the horrors of twentieth-century warfare. This is the last we see of either of them.

The crossed-out opening paragraph of chapter 10 in the handwritten manuscript of the novel begins: "There are only three people of any importance in this story although my life was full of people, all of whom were important at the time." After this midpoint of the novel two of them disappear—I would argue, because they can no longer contribute to the education of Frederic Henry. A third character has emerged who embodies the *useful* qualities of each of them. Catherine Barkley is the synthesis of the priest's faith in an ideal of love and service tempered by a Rinaldi-like cynicism, an impatience with platitude and illusion, and a good-humored relish for sensation. She is the closest thing we have in this novel to a "code hero."

By the time we meet Catherine she already has been "initiated." She had become a field nurse harboring the romantic notion that her fiancé might come to the hospital where she was: "With a sabre cut, I suppose, and a bandage around his head. Or shot through the shoulder. Something picturesque," she tells Frederic. Instead he was "blown to bits" and with him Catherine's faith in abstract ideals. "Far from being a blind romantic, she is a shellshocked victim of the war," in Wexler's words, and her willingness to submerge herself in her relationship with Frederic, far from being a sign of female spinelessness, is an act of will. Reeling from her losses, Catherine is now determined to forge a meaningful existence for herself in a world where the traditional structures—morality, religion, patriotism—have proven hollow and empty, even "obscene."

Jackson Benson describes Frederic in his early encounters with Catherine as a "casual, uniformed boy on the make" as he sets out to take a girl "as part of the game that every young, virile lad must play." Frederic himself conceives of their early encounters as "a game, like bridge, in which you said things instead of playing cards." The irony is that while he thinks he is playing with Catherine, he is blithely oblivious to the fact that she is using *him*.

Catherine knows exactly what is going on, and she has enough self-respect to find the "nurse's evening off aspect of it" distasteful. Her awareness of the pretense of their situation is obvious from their very first conversation. After a few sentences of meaningless exchange, she interrupts him, saying, "*Do* we have to go on and talk this way?" She proceeds immediately to tell this stranger of the death of the man she was going to marry and of her regret that she hadn't slept with him before he was killed.

A few days later, only the third time she has seen Frederic, she initiates a strange dialogue:

> "Say, 'I've come back to Catherine in the night.'"
> "I've come back to Catherine in the night."
> "Oh, darling, you have come back, haven't you?"

But a moment later, after a long kiss, "She came back from wherever she had been" and coldly pronounces, "This is a rotten game we play, isn't it?" "What game?" he replies. "Don't be dull," she answers, and his disingenuousness looks merely foolish when confronted by her honesty.

"You're a nice boy. . . . And you play it as well as you know how. But it's a rotten game. . . . Please let's not lie when we don't have to. I had a very fine little show and I'm all right now. You see I'm not mad and I'm not gone off. It's only a little sometimes." When he presses her hand and says, "Dear Catherine," she says, "It sounds very funny now— Catherine. You don't pronounce it very much alike." And suddenly we begin to understand what must have been taking place in her mind when she made Frederic pronounce the words she wished so desperately she could hear from her dead lover that she had planted them in the mouth of a stranger.

Catherine is playing at love not for diversion but survival. Hers is a sophisticated game, over his head, and Frederic does not understand the stakes. When Frederic returns home afterward, Rinaldi observes an erosion in the chess player's confidence:

> "Ah, ha!" he said. "It does not go so well. Baby is puzzled. . . . Where have you been?"
> "Calling on the British."
> "Thank God I did not become involved with the British."

Later, in Milan, Catherine tells Frederic, "When I met you perhaps I was nearly crazy. Perhaps I was crazy. But now we're happy and we love each other." She herself puts it in problem-solution terms. Aware of the precariousness of her own sanity, Catherine has made a deliberate retreat into a private existence of her own construction, where, by scrupulously acting out a role, she can order her world and achieve some semblance of self-determination. (We have witnessed Nick Adams, back from the war, employing the same psychological survival skill in "Big Two-Hearted River," keeping tight rein on his troubled thoughts as he attends meticulously to the details of trout fishing.) "We're going to have a strange life," she had pronounced cryptically the first time they kissed, thereby taking control, and casting Frederic—compliant, convenient, and quite unsuspecting—as substitute player for her boy who was killed. Eventually both she and Frederic will grow into their parts until they are no longer acting, but it should not be forgotten that in this little play, not only is Catherine the romantic heroine, but from the beginning, she was producer and director as well.

II

From the moment she pulls herself together and defines the perimeters of her own existence, Catherine exemplifies the Hemingway code.

She lives for the moment and cares nothing for convention. Her faith is in the validity of her own emotions. She regrets having "saved herself" for marriage: "He could have had anything he wanted if I would have known," she tells Frederic. "I didn't know about anything then." It is Frederic who, upon learning Catherine is pregnant, thinks that they probably ought to get married. But Catherine is beyond that stage: "But darling," she explains, "I am married. I'm married to you. . . . You see, darling, I had one experience of waiting to be married." If not older, she is wiser than our "Hemingway hero," and that has made her, like other "code heroes," a simpler kind of person. As she later explains to Frederic, "Life isn't hard to manage when you've nothing to lose."

Catherine is cynical and unimpressed by conventional postures of power and prestige. Having had the man she loved blown to bits, she is disgusted by military trappings that serve to glorify war. She cannot stand Ettore, the "legitimate hero." "You can picture him at the front and you know he's useful," she tells Frederic, "but he's so much the type of boy I don't care for." Frederic, who can still be impressed that Ettore is about to be a captain, asks if she wouldn't like him to have some more exalted rank, but her attitude is purely pragmatic: "No, darling. I only want you to have enough rank so that we're admitted to the better restaurants." When Frederic pours a water glass a third full of cognac and drinks it off, she punctures his show: "That was very big," she said. "I know brandy is for heroes. But you shouldn't exaggerate."

Of the British major who had declared "we were all cooked," Frederic had noted that "there was a great contrast between his world pessimism and personal cheeriness." The code demands a lust for life and a cheerful disregard of doom. As Frederic and Catherine row across Lago Maggiore to Switzerland in the dark and rain, she has no illusions about their situation. When Frederic warns her to watch that the oar doesn't strike her in the stomach, she wryly replies, "If it did, life might be much simpler." Yet she maintains her "personal cheeriness," annoying Frederic by laughing at how funny he had looked holding an open umbrella by the edges as they tried to use it as a sail. Fetching him a drink of water from the choppy lake with the bailing pail, she replies to his thank-you with black humor: "You're ever so welcome. . . . There's much more if you want it." She gets through the ordeal by thinking all night of the wonderful breakfast rolls they have in Switzerland, and even in the midst of her protracted labor, enjoys getting "drunk" on the anaesthetic gas. ("I'm a fool about the gas. It's wonderful," she says, and Frederic retorts, "We'll have to get some for the home.") Conversation between the two is often marked by an understated comic irony, fetching the part of Rinaldi that is sane into the very spirit of their sacramental love affair.

By code standards, her stoicism is exemplary. Her ability to overcome a bad moment of feeling like a whore in a red plush Milan hotel room just before Frederic leaves for the front is testament to her ability to reshape her surroundings by force of will and to her determination to play the best she can with the hand she is dealt. When Frederic asks if she can remember who said "the coward dies a thousand deaths, the brave but one," Catherine corrects the statement: "The brave dies perhaps two thousand deaths if he's intelligent. He simply doesn't mention them," she says. Throughout her labor she wants "to have this child without any foolishness." When her own death is imminent she says, "I'm not afraid. I just hate it," and winking at Frederic, her face gray, speaks her final words: "Don't worry, darling. . . . I'm not a bit afraid. It's just a dirty trick."

Frederic is profoundly affected by his relationship with Catherine. Rinaldi observed a change in him immediately upon his return from Milan and disapproved: "You act like a married man," he tells Frederic. "What's the matter with you? . . . Oh, baby how you've come back to me. You come back serious and with a liver. I tell you this war is a bad thing." Frederic now has a "sacred subject."

By the time he and Catherine have established their separate peace in Switzerland, Frederic is sounding a lot like Catherine Barkley: "If you aren't with me, I haven't a thing in the world," and "I'm no good when you're not there. I haven't any life at all any more," he tells her. Whether such exclusive dependency on another is healthy for a man *or* a woman is another matter altogether, and some have demonstrated why it is not. Millicent Bell calls them "Hemingway's pitiful pair," moving in their isolation toward an almost animal-like state of numbness and ennui. But the point here is that by the end of the novel, Frederic is as deeply immersed in this relationship as Catherine, who has borne all the criticism for it. And given the treacherousness of Hemingway's world, the consequences of structuring one's existence within the confines of a love relationship seem hardly less "healthy" than living by the rituals that other code heroes have chosen in order to structure their lives—the bullfight, the prizefight, the hunt. Certainly it is not as deadly by definition as what Frederic and Catherine have sought to escape: war.

The Hemingway code is a survival tactic, and Hemingway's is ultimately a world at war: "one in which things do not grow and bear fruit, but explode, break, decompose, or are eaten away." Clearly, it is a limited vision, "a world seen through a crack in a wall by a man who is pinned down by gunfire," and critics often have objected to it. "It is a hell of a world and we should protest it," says Young. "But on the other hand we should be hard pressed to prove it is not the one we inhabit." It is to Catherine Barkley's credit that she has found a way to live in it.

The priest had told Frederic that when you love you wish to serve, to do things for, and in his final hours with Catherine, Frederic assumes this role of service quite literally, administering the gas to relieve her pain and thinking, "It was very good of the doctor to let me do something." And we see Catherine, the "initiated" one of the pair, trying to prepare him for life after her death. "I'll come and stay with you nights," she says. In that line she echoes her own request of Frederic in one of their first encounters, when she had asked him to say, "I've come back to Catherine in the night," trying to ease her grief by pretending that he was her own dead lover come back to her. Frederic's sense of the futility of trying to say goodbye to a statue when he is alone in the hospital room with her body is hardly proof that he ultimately cared little for Catherine, a negation of the value of their love, as some have suggested. Frederic simply is too much a realist to sentimentalize a corpse, and in that respect, he again is following Catherine's example. With brutal frankness she had told the horrible facts of her fiancé's death, and she had refused to indulge in any hope of an afterlife. "That was the end of it," she had told Frederic, and when he had attempted consolation by saying, "I don't know," she had replied firmly, "Oh yes, that's the end of it."

"Do you always know what people think?" Frederic had asked Catherine after she first pronounced theirs a "rotten game." "Not always. But I do with you," she replied. Catherine *knows:* that Frederic at first views their encounters as a chess game in which she is the prize, that he is only pretending as he responds dutifully to her cues to profess his love, that they will have a strange life, that she will be dead in the rain. Her powers of prescience might be read as female intuition, some mysterious form of extra-rational perception, further reinforcing the common view of her as an idealized representation of the female principle. (In fact, Dekker and Harris, the only critics who have examined "the submerged folkloristic motifs of second sight and revenants" in the novel, characterize the relationship between Catherine and Frederic as an unresolved "dialectic" between female faith and male skepticism.) But I believe that Catherine's ability to penetrate surfaces and to read the inevitabilities of the future underscores her stature as the wiser, more experienced of the pair, whose role it is to educate Frederic Henry.

Michael Reynolds has noted that Frederic displays an insider's knowledge of continental travel that leads him directly to the right hotels and restaurants, where, if not known already, he gains the instant respect and trust of desk clerks and barmen who unhesitatingly offer him clothing, papers, safe haven, or rowboats for midnight trips to Switzerland. "At no time in the novel does he appear a novice. . . . The reader never sees him learning to do anything; he already knows." According to Reynolds, this saves Hemingway a lot of explaining and at the same time establishes Frederic's credibility: "The reader is willing to accept much of Frederic's knowledge because he has been presented as the insider who understands the territory." But if Frederic knows the physical landscape of the novel— how to move about in a foreign country at war, where to go, what to order, and how to order it—Catherine knows the emotional territory. She's been there before. And this insider's knowledge establishes *her* credibility as Frederic's mentor in matters of psychological survival.

In Frederic's retrospective narrative, we can see the extent to which his having loved Catherine has shaped his character and values. The famous passage on bravery, the one that F. Scott Fitzgerald thought was so fine that Hemingway should use it to end the book, is triggered by Frederic's memory of her: "If people bring so much courage to this world the world has to kill them to break them, so of course it kills them. The world breaks everyone and afterward many are strong at the broken places." Catherine's pronouncement as she faces her own death, "They've broken me," is embedded at the core of this passage on the nature of courage that reflects the mature Frederic's very philosophy of life.

III

But why has Catherine, the only character besides Frederic Henry who inhabits this novel from beginning to end, been so consistently ignored as a model of the Hemingway code? The simplest explanation is that it probably has never occurred to most readers that the "code hero" could be a woman. The language of the critics is revealing. Philip Young defines the code as "made of the controls of honor and courage which in a life of tension and pain make a man a man." Earl Rovit, borrowing the terms of Hemingway's Colonel Cantwell, calls the code hero "a 'tough boy'—a man who will make his play and then back it up. Or just a man who backs his play." James Light has observed that in Hemingway's world humanity's problem is to "learn to dominate death as the bullfighter's is to dominate the bull, and the way toward domination is to see life, like the bullfight, as an art form with certain rules the manly man will obey." We have been conditioned to expect that the game, the ordering ritual, will be a traditionally masculine one—the bullfight, the card game, the boxing match, the big game hunt. It is little wonder that we have overlooked Nurse Barkley, the beautiful blonde in a predominantly female profession and an exclusively female condition, whose game of choice, about the only one a woman could play, is love.

Catherine also has been attacked or dismissed for her simplicity. But the code hero, the exemplar, usually *is* a simple character. Earl Rovit notes that "the tutor is a much less complicated figure than the tyro; but he is certainly no more realistic." He is less reflective, less consciously aware of his acts, less burdened by troubling reflection and imagining, than the young man to whom he serves as an example. He is "'a simpler man.' He is so simple, in fact, that he is closer to brute animality than 'humanness.'"

Nor should it be forgotten that we are dealing here with a writer who wanted to write the way Cézanne painted, a writer who thought that the dignity of movement of an iceberg is due to only one-eighth of it being above water. True, we know little about Catherine Barkley beyond what Frederic thinks about her and what Hemingway reveals in dialogue, but what do we know of Frederic, except that he had been in Italy studying architecture and that he corresponds with his family infrequently?

But another problem many readers may have had in taking Catherine Barkley seriously is that it is hard for them to see the subordination of the individual ego to a personal relationship as a mark of maturity. Rather than being respected for her self-knowledge and clear-eyed pragmatism as she attempts to construct a sane context for her existence in an insane world, Catherine has been perceived as lacking in character because she has chosen to define herself in terms of a relationship. "There isn't any me anymore. Just what you want," she tells Frederic, and later, "You're my religion. You're all I've got." The wise and worldly Count Greffi had sanctioned the ideal when he had reminded Frederic not to forget that love is a religious feeling. Few critics have argued with this insight or with the priest's definition of love as the desire to serve, but many have been critical of Catherine when she puts this ethic into practice in a secular context. Daniel Schneider describes Catherine as "despair turning desperately to the religion of love," obviously seeing no strength in that "religion." Richard Hovey writes: "Such a disvaluing of Catherine of her own self, such a need to flee the normal burdens of selfhood, indicates that her love is feverish in its dependency." Such views may tell us more about the values of critics and our culture than they do about Catherine Barkley, and the gender bias revealed in the diction of critics who have devalued her or ignored her as the exemplar of the novel may be far more deeply embedded in their thinking than we have realized.

Carol Gilligan, in her widely discussed book entitled *In a Different Voice: Psychological Theory and Women's Development* (Harvard University Press, 1982), explores why, in terms of widely accepted psychological theories of moral development, a disproportionate number of women seem to be "stuck" at a stage at which morality is conceived in interpersonal terms and goodness equated with helping and pleasing others. At the higher stages, according to prevailing theory, concern with particulars of relationships is subordinated to rules and finally, rules to universal principles of justice. In a scheme that defines moral development in terms of individuation and individual achievement and that equates maturity with personal autonomy, "concern with relationships appears as a weakness of women rather than as a human strength." But, she argues, "the failure of women to fit existing models of human growth may point to a problem in the representation." Gilligan calls for a more balanced view of moral development that will accord equal respect to both modes of thinking that she has observed, modes which for purposes of differentiation in her discussion, she terms "masculine" and "feminine"—the "masculine" conceiving of morality in terms of a hierarchy of abstract principles and the "feminine" making moral judgments in the context of particular relationships of care.

The Garden of Eden, posthumously edited and published by Scribner's in 1986, has kindled the issue of Hemingway's "androgyny." But talk so far has focused on the length of haircuts, on hints of unconventional sexual practices, and on the author's supposed attraction to boylike women. But if we accept Gilligan's terminology, then Hemingway's "androgyny" may exist on a far more profound level—in the values that his characters can believe in and live by. The author of *A Farewell to Arms* does nothing to undercut Catherine's assertion when she declares her relationship with Frederic the sole source of meaning for her in the universe, saying, "there's only us two and in the world there's all the rest of them. If anything comes between us we're gone and then they have us."

Gilligan also observes that what she terms the feminine mode of thinking involves "a contextual judgment, bound to particulars of time and place, contingent upon the details of the situation and resisting a categorical formation." Frederic feels that "abstract words such as glory, honor, courage, or hallow were obscene beside the concrete names of villages, the numbers of roads, the names of rivers, the numbers of regiments and the dates." Scott Donaldson notes in all of Hemingway's protagonists "a disinclination to philosophize, much": "They learn from experience and distrust abstract generalization." And this "contextual" mode of judgment sounds very much like the approach to morality that Hemingway articulated for himself in *Death in the Afternoon,* explaining (although not defending) his inability to intellectualize an abstract scheme of morality: "So far, about morals, I know only that what is moral is what you feel good after and what is immoral is what you feel bad after."

Catherine's death and the consequent destruction of the lovers' "separate peace" are not proof of Hemingway's misogyny, his subconscious desire to kill off the threat to masculine freedom that Catherine, the quintessential female, represents, as some have argued. Judith Fetterley reads *A Farewell to Arms* as Hemingway's "resentful cryptogram" of hostility toward women—another expression of the inability of male American authors to deal with a mature heterosexual relationship. Leslie Fiedler, too, believes that "Hemingway is only really comfortable in dealing with 'men without women'" and asserts, "Had Catherine lived, she could only have turned into a bitch; for this is the fate in Hemingway's imagination of all Anglo-Saxon women." In Hemingway's world the casualty figures are high, and certainly not all—not even many—of the victims are female. Catherine's death is an artistic necessity if *A Farewell to Arms* is to be an articulation of Hemingway's tragic vision that "the world breaks everyone."

Catherine and Frederic lead an accelerated and abstracted existence, and the author himself said in his next book, published three years later, "If two people love each other there can be no happy end to it" (*Death in the Afternoon*). He applied the philosophy explicitly to *A Farewell to Arms* in his introduction to the 1948 illustrated edition when he wrote, "The fact that the book was a tragic one did not make me unhappy since I believed that life was a tragedy and knew it could only have one end." The *Farewell to Arms* manuscripts in the John F. Kennedy Library show Hemingway was not exaggerating when he told George Plimpton that he rewrote the conclusion of the novel thirty-nine times before he was satisfied. Bernard Oldsey has catalogued the variants, which, along with a few Miscellaneous Endings, he refers to as The *Nada* Ending, The Fitzgerald Ending, The Religious Ending, The Live-Baby Ending, The Morning-After Ending, The Funeral Ending, The Original *Scribner's Magazine* Ending, and *The* Ending. In none of them does Catherine survive. Through Catherine's death and the death of the private system of meaning that she and Frederic have crafted for themselves through their love, Hemingway presents us with the regrettable fact that in terms of what values will survive, it is still, in Gilligan's representation, a "man's world." That does not necessarily mean he prefers it that way.

IV

But finally, what do we do with the famous Hemingway machismo? Some would argue that our knowledge of the author must preclude any reading that would place a woman in a role to be emulated by a man. But it would be a mistake to accept the carefully cultivated public persona of "Papa Hemingway" as the full explanation of the man, and in the case of any writer, it is important to keep the line straight between the artist and the art. Kay Boyle, whose own early work was appearing alongside Hemingway's in the little magazines published in Paris in the 1920s, had far less trouble than most of us today in distinguishing the man from his work. (Clearly she preferred the latter.) She wrote to a friend in 1931, "I read Farewell to Arms the other night and had another good cry over Catherine. As for Hemingway, I think him unspeakable. He has no right to have such a wonderful woman as Catherine. Perhaps he made her up, because he knew he could never have anyone so wonderful."

Despite the Hemingway legend, reading Catherine Barkley as a strong character is not inconsistent with the biographical "facts" anyway. Agnes von Kurowsky, commonly acknowledged as a primary prototype for Catherine, was seven years Hemingway's senior when he met her in the Red Cross hospital in Milan after being wounded in 1918. She was a self-possessed professional woman, proud of being a *Bellevue*-educated nurse. A letter she wrote to Ernest in December 1918 indicates that theirs was a fun-loving relationship of equals, and in its affectionate, playful tone, could have been written by Catherine Barkley: "Kid, we're going to be partners. So if you are going to drink, I am too. Just the same amount." Agnes was sweet and gentle but no pushover; a good sport who firmly resisted any unwanted advances from the soldiers in her charge while remaining the favorite of all; and it was *she* who proved to pull the strings in their relationship, breaking Ernest's heart by becoming engaged to an Italian officer after the teenaged ambulance driver had gone home to Oak Park. Nor were the other "Hemingway women" lacking in character or stature. Hadley Richardson, his first wife, also was significantly older than he, by eight years. And his three other wives, Pauline Pfeiffer, Martha Gellhorn, and Mary Welsh, all were independent professional women—writers—themselves when he met them.

But it is safer to look to a writer's work than to his life. *The Garden of Eden* challenges the stereotypical Hemingway machismo in its portrait of David Bourne, a young writer with habits of composition identical to his creator's, down to writing in the mornings in cheap school notebooks: he harbors deep misgivings about a big game hunt he had witnessed as a child, and he rather passively goes along with the sex role reversals his wife desires, letting her be the "boy" and accepting into their relationship another woman to whom she is attracted. More importantly here, the book may also reveal some undercurrents in Hemingway's conception of Catherine Barkley. The heroine of *The Garden of Eden* ultimately proves to be a radically different kind of woman: she really *is* crazy, with no dead fiancé to explain it, and she seems to pursue quite earnestly her stated intention to "ruin" her husband, incinerating the only copy of his work in progress. But nevertheless, she bears some striking resemblances to Catherine Barkley—in her manner of speech, in her desire to be "one person" with her man, in her determination to retreat into a private world of love, even in her name: Catherine Bourne.

The echoes reverberate throughout the novel. "There's only us two and in the world there's all the rest of them," says Catherine Barkley; "You know you must never worry about me because I love you and we're us against all the others," Catherine Bourne tells David. Catherine Barkley wants Frederic to let his hair grow and to get her own cut so that they can be "just alike only one of us blonde and one of us dark." Catherine Bourne *does* get her hair cut like a boy's and furthermore persuades David to visit her coiffeur and have his cut and bleached identically. She is delighted when people mistake them for brother and sister.

But a far more significant parallel is that both women have defined their own private realities and within those narrow bounds act out their lives like parts in a play. Catherine Bourne states explicitly what Hemingway never allows Catherine Barkley to articulate (and makes a Freudian slip as she does it): "When you start to live outside yourself," she tells David, "it's all dangerous. Maybe I'd better go back into our world, your and my world that I made up; we made up I mean. I was a great success in that world." She recognizes the dangers of such solipsism when she says, "I was thinking so much about myself that I was getting impossible again, like a painter and I was my own picture." The problem in *The Garden of Eden* is that the rules by which Catherine Barkley attempts to order her existence in a world gone mad are themselves mad when applied to a leisurely honeymoon existence on the French Riviera. When Catherine Bourne attempts to live her life as art, it is destructive and escapist self-indulgence. When, like Hemingway's other traumatized victims of war, Catherine Barkley does it, it is a desperate but heroic effort at survival.

Finally, the manuscripts of *A Farewell to Arms* also support the reading of Catherine Barkley as the initiated one and of Frederic Henry as the young apprentice with much to learn. Hemingway wrote in *Death in the Afternoon,* "If a writer of prose knows enough about what he is writing about he may omit things that he knows and the reader, if the writer is writing truly enough, will have a feeling of those things as strongly as though the writer had stated them." The young writer-protagonist of *The Garden of Eden* echoes the aesthetic: "Be careful, he said to himself, it is all very well for you to write simply and the simpler the better. But do not start to think so damned simply. Know how complicated it is and then state it simply." The handwritten manuscript of the novel shows Hemingway's iceberg theory in practice. If in the case of other writers we might logically assume that they crossed things out because they had not said exactly what they had meant, in Hemingway's case we often find that he deletes material because it states *too* exactly what he meant. Consistently he revises toward leanness and understatement.

In the manuscript version Frederic appears less experienced, less in control than in the finished novel. Immediately following Catherine's pronouncement that "we're going to have a strange life," Hemingway crossed out this sentence: "I did not know what it was all about." In the final paragraph of that chapter Frederic again appears curiously passive, very much the "little puppy" that Rinaldi calls him. Hemingway drew a line through this sentence: "I did not know what it was all about with Katherine Barkley but it was out of my control." In the sentences he let stand in the manuscript, Frederic is still confused but slightly more cavalier: "In bed I lay awake a long time. I did not know what it was all about but it was something to do." The published version of chapter 5 closes with the simple sentences of description preceding both tries: "I knocked over his candle with the pillow and got into bed in the dark. Rinaldi picked up the candle, lit it and went on reading." At the end of chapter 7, after Frederic says he had gotten somewhat drunk and treated seeing Catherine very lightly, yet finds himself feeling empty and hollow when he learns he cannot see her, Hemingway deletes an explication of Frederic's confusion and a strong hint at how significant a force Catherine will prove to be:

> I had nearly forgotten to come but when I could not see her
>   suddenly lonely. Something I did not know
> I felt ~~very badly terribly. It was a first small unheeded~~
> about was going on all right
> ~~warning of how things could be.~~
>   ~~felt as though I had missed something very important~~

The manuscript also supports the reading that in their early encounters Catherine is acting a part and has a script in mind for her leading man as well, even though Frederic cannot realize the full implication of what he senses. Just after their first meeting, chapter 4 of the published novel closes with these lines:

> After a while we said good-night and left. Walking home Rinaldi said, "Miss Barkley prefers you to me. That is very clear. But the little Scotch one is very nice."
> "Very," I said. I had not noticed her. "You like her?"
> "No," said Rinaldi.

Chapter 4 of the manuscript ends:

> "Very," I said. I had not noticed her. *I felt I had been talking a part in a bad play* [italics mine].

What Hemingway edited out of the early encounters between Catherine and Frederic in the manuscript delineates more obviously than he must have wished the role of Catherine as the director of a drama the young man does not understand.

V

"Women read men more truly than men read women," declares the protagonist of Charlotte Brontë's *Shirley*, and she intends the observation both of life and of literature. *A Farewell to Arms* bears her out. Within the novel, Catherine certainly is the more perceptive of the pair. She immediately sees through Frederic's "chess game" while silently employing him for far more complicated purposes of her own. He does not begin to grasp what is going on; it never crosses his mind that she could be anything more than the object of his intentions. Frederic misreads Catherine, blinded by his assumptions about women. So, too, critics have misread her, their vision obscured, if not by assumptions about women, then by assumptions about Hemingway's women.

Even feminist critics have viewed Catherine as nothing more than a projection of the male imagination. Judith Fetterley concludes that "Catherine's contradictions are *not* resolvable, because her character is determined by forces outside her; it is a reflection of male psychology and male fantasy life and is understandable only when seen as a series of responses to the needs of the male world that surrounds her." Joyce Wexler, I believe, is quite right when she counters, "While these statements reflect Fetterley's analysis of women in patriarchal literature, they do not, unfortunately, describe Hemingway's novel accurately." Accepting Catherine Barkley as simply the antithesis of Frederic incorporates and perpetuates the very paradigm that most feminist critics would oppose.

A theoretical approach that may prove more useful than others in reading this particular novel is outlined by Adrienne Munich, who argues that feminist critics should not dedicate themselves exclusively to recovering works written by women or to reviling biased portrayals of women in works written by men: "This view reinforces the way things are, with women inhabiting the margins of power. In [Toni] Morrison's words, this is 'a whiney tale'—a truth that peaks somewhere between anger and a desire for comfort." Instead, she calls for fresh and challenging readings of traditional texts "encrusted with patriarchal interpretations" (*Making a Difference: Feminist Literary Criticism,* edited by Gayle Greene and Coppélia Kahn). If ever there was a book "encrusted with patriarchal interpretations," *A Farewell to Arms* is it. "Traditional literary works carry stories of a two-sexed world where difference has been mythologized and hierarchized but where other knowledge in the same texts subverts those categories. The canon has been owned by a monopoly, but acts of repossession have begun," Munich writes. "In the background of patriarchal texts are women trying to escape into readability." I believe that Catherine Barkley is one of them.

As much a victim of the war as her boy who was killed, her ideals shattered and her psyche scarred in confrontation with a chaotic and hostile universe, Catherine refuses to be helpless. She pulls herself together with dignity and grace, defines the limits of her own existence, and scrupulously acts her part, preferring romance to the theater of the absurd. By imposing an order on experience, she gains a limited autonomy, as much control over her own destiny as a human being in Hemingway's world can hope to have. From her example, Frederic Henry learns how to live in it too.

A question remains: Did Hemingway *intend* Catherine Barkley as the manifestation of the "Hemingway code," the controls of courage and honor he so admired? Ultimately the work must speak for itself. In *Death in the Afternoon* Hemingway described his struggle to capture in his writing "the real thing, the sequence of motion and fact which made the emotion and which would be as valid in a year or in ten years, or, with luck and if you stated it purely enough, always." Catherine Barkley is the "real thing." In creating her, he was more successful than perhaps he knew and than most of his critics have realized.

Chronology

1899   Hemingway born July 21 in Oak Park, Illinois.

1917   Works as reporter on *Kansas City Star*.

1918   Service in Italy with the American Red Cross; wounded on July 8 near Fossalta di Piave; affair with nurse Agnes von Kurowsky.

1920   Reporter for *Toronto Star*.

1921   Marries Hadley Richardson; moves to Paris.

1922   Reports Greco-Turkish War for *Toronto Star*.

1923   *Three Stories and Ten Poems* published in Paris.

1924   A collection of vignettes, *in our time*, published in Paris by three mountains press.

1925   Attends Fiesta de San Fermin in Pamplona with Harold Loeb, Pat Guthrie, Duff Twysden, and others. *In Our Time*, which adds fourteen short stories to the earlier vignettes, is published in New York by Horace Liveright. It is Hemingway's first American book.

1926   *The Torrents of Spring* and *The Sun Also Rises* published by Charles Scribner's Sons.

1927   *Men without Women* published. Marries Pauline Pfeiffer.

1928   Moves to Key West.

1929   *A Farewell to Arms* published.

1932   *Death in the Afternoon* published.

1933   *Winner Take Nothing* published.

1935   *Green Hills of Africa* published.

1937   *To Have and Have Not* published. Returns to Spain as war correspondent on the Loyalist side.

1938   Writes script for the film *The Spanish Earth*. *The Fifth Column and the First Forty-Nine Stories* published.

1940   Marries Martha Gellhorn. *For Whom the Bell Tolls* published. Buys house in Cuba where he lives throughout most of the 1940s and 1950s.

1942   Edits *Men at War.*

1944   Takes part in Allied liberation of Paris with partisan unit.

1946   Marries Mary Welsh.

1950   *Across the River and into the Trees* published.

1952   *The Old Man and the Sea* published.

1954   Receives Nobel Prize for literature for *The Old Man and the Sea.*

1960   Settles in Ketchum, Idaho.

1961   Commits suicide on July 2, in Ketchum.

1964   *A Moveable Feast* published.

1970   *Islands in the Stream* published.

1986   *The Garden of Eden* published.

Contributors

HAROLD BLOOM, Sterling Professor of the Humanities at Yale University, is the author of *The Anxiety of Influence, Poetry and Repression,* and many other volumes of literary criticism. His forthcoming study, *Freud: Transference and Authority,* attempts a full-scale reading of all of Freud's major writings. A MacArthur Prize Fellow, he is general editor of five series of literary criticism published by Chelsea House. During 1987–88, he was appointed Charles Eliot Norton Professor of Poetry at Harvard University.

DANIEL J. SCHNEIDER is Professor of English at the University of Tennessee in Knoxville. His books include *The Consciousness of D. H. Lawrence: An Intellectual Biography, The Crystal Cage: Adventures of the Imagination in the Fiction of Henry James,* and *Symbolism: The Manichean Vision: A Study in the Art of James, Conrad, Woolf, and Stevens.*

ROBERT MERRILL is Professor of English at the University of Nevada, Reno, and the author of numerous scholarly articles on twentieth-century American literature.

WILLIAM ADAIR is Professor of English at the University of Utah at Salt Lake City. He has published several essays on the works of Ernest Hemingway.

MICHAEL S. REYNOLDS is Professor of English at North Carolina State University. He is the author of *Hemingway's First War: The Making of A Farewell to Arms, Hemingway's Reading, 1910–1940,* and the recent acclaimed biography, *The Young Hemingway.*

JUDITH FETTERLEY is Professor of English at the State University of New York, Albany. She is the author of *The Resisting Reader: A Feminist Approach to American Fiction* as well as of a number of articles treating the sexual politics of American literature.

BERNARD OLDSEY is Professor of English at West Chester University in West Chester, Pennsylvania. He is best known for his scholarly essays on Ernest Hemingway.

SCOTT DONALDSON is a former faculty member of the College of William and Mary. He is the author of *The Life and Art of Ernest Hemingway* and of books on Winfield Townley Scott and F. Scott Fitzgerald. His most recent work is *Conversations with John Cheever.*

MILLICENT BELL is Professor of English at Boston University. She has published *Hawthorne's View of the Artist, Edith Wharton and Henry James: The Story of Their Friendship,* and *Marquand: An American Life,* which received the Winship Prize and was nominated for the National Book Award in biography.

SANDRA WHIPPLE SPANIER is Assistant Professor of English at Oregon State University. The author of a critical biography, *Kay Boyle: Artist and Activist,* Spanier has also published articles on Hemingway, Salinger, Lawrence, Hawthorne, and Poe.

Bibliography

Baker, Carlos. *Hemingway: The Writer as Artist*. Princeton: Princeton University Press, 1952.

———, ed. *Ernest Hemingway: Selected Letters, 1917–1961*. New York: Scribner's, 1981.

———, ed. *Hemingway and His Critics: An International Anthology*. New York: Hill & Wang, 1961.

———, ed. *Hemingway: Critiques of Four Major Novels*. New York: Scribner's, 1962.

Baker, Sheridan. *Ernest Hemingway: An Introduction and Interpretation*. New York: Holt, Rinehart, 1967.

Balbert, Peter. "From Hemingway to Lawrence to Mailer: Survival and Sexual Identity in *A Farewell to Arms*." *Hemingway Review* 3, no. 1 (1983): 30–43.

Benson, Jackson J. *Hemingway: The Writer's Art of Self-Defense*. Minneapolis: University of Minnesota Press, 1969.

Brenner, Gerry. *Concealments in Hemingway's Works*. Columbus: Ohio State University Press, 1983.

Bruccoli, Matthew J. *Scott and Ernest: The Authority of Failure and the Authority of Success*. New York: Random House, 1978.

Burke, Kenneth. *A Grammar of Motives* and *A Rhetoric of Motives*. 2 vol. ed. Cleveland: World Publishing, 1962.

Cecil, L. Moffitt. "The Color of *A Farewell to Arms*." *Research Studies* 36 (June 1968): 168–73.

Cooperman, Stanley. "Death and *Cojones:* Hemingway's *A Farewell to Arms*." *The South Atlantic Quarterly* 63 (1964): 85–92.

Cowley, Malcolm. "Not Yet Demobilized." *New York Review of Books,* 6 October 1929, 6.

———, ed. *Viking Portable Hemingway*. New York: Viking, 1944.

D'Avanzo, Mario L. "The Motif of Corruption in *A Farewell to Arms*." *Lock Haven Review* 11 (1969): 57–62.

Davis, Robert M. "'If You Did Not Go Forward': Process and Stasis in *A Farewell to Arms*." *Studies in the Novel* 2 (1970): 305–11.

Dekker, George, and Joseph Harris. "Supernaturalism and the Vernacular Style in *A Farewell to Arms*." *PMLA* 94 (1979): 311–18.

Donaldson, Scott. *By Force of Will: The Life and Art of Ernest Hemingway*. New York: Viking, 1977.

Eby, Cecil D. "The *Soul* of Ernest Hemingway." *Studies in American Fiction* 12 (1984): 223–26.

Engelberg, Edward. "Hemingway's 'True Penelope': Flaubert's *L'Education Sentimentale* and *A Farewell to Arms.*" *Comparative Literature Studies* 16 (1979): 180–216.

Fiedler, Leslie A. *Love and Death in the American Novel.* Rev. ed. New York: Stein & Day, 1975.

Fleming, Robert E. "Hemingway and Peele: Chapter 1 of *A Farewell to Arms.*" *Studies in American Fiction* 11 (1983): 95–100.

Ganzel, Dewey. "*A Farewell to Arms:* The Danger of Imagination." *The Sewanee Review* 79 (1971): 576–97.

Gelfant, Blanche. "Language as a Moral Code in *A Farewell to Arms.*" *Modern Fiction Studies* 9 (1963): 173–76.

Gellens, Jay, ed. *Twentieth Century Interpretations of* A Farewell to Arms: *A Collection of Critical Essays.* Englewood Cliffs, N.J.: Prentice-Hall, 1970.

Gerstenberger, Donna. "The Waste Land in *A Farewell to Arms.*" *MLN* 76 (1961): 24–25.

Glasser, William A. "*A Farewell to Arms.*" *The Sewanee Review* 74 (1966): 453–67.

Grebstein, Sheldon. *Hemingway's Craft.* Carbondale: Southern Illinois University Press, 1973.

Griffin, Peter. *Along with Youth: Hemingway, the Early Years.* Oxford: Oxford University Press, 1985.

Grimes, Larry E. *The Religious Design of Hemingway's Early Fiction.* Ann Arbor: UMI Research Press, 1985.

Gurko, Leo. *Ernest Hemingway and the Pursuit of Heroism.* New York: Crowell, 1968.

Hackett, Francis. "Hemingway: *A Farewell to Arms.*" *Saturday Review of Literature,* 6 August 1949, 32–33.

Hanneman, Audre. *Ernest Hemingway: A Comprehensive Bibliography.* Princeton: Princeton University Press, 1967.

———. *Supplement to* Ernest Hemingway: A Comprehensive Bibliography. Princeton: Princeton University Press, 1975.

Hovey, Richard B. "*A Farewell to Arms:* Hemingway's *Liebstod.*" *University Review* 33 (Winter 1966, Spring 1967): 93–100, 163–68.

———. *Hemingway: The Inward Terrain.* Seattle: University of Washington Press, 1968.

Keeler, Clinton. "*A Farewell to Arms:* Hemingway and Peele." *MLN* 76 (1961): 622–25.

Kert, Bernice. *The Hemingway Women.* New York: Norton, 1983.

Killinger, John. *Hemingway and the Dead Gods: A Study in Existentialism.* Lexington: University of Kentucky Press, 1961.

Kobler, J. F. "Let's Run Catherine Barkley Up the Flag Pole and See Who Salutes." *CEA Critic* 36 (1974): 4–10.

Lee, A. Robert, ed. *Ernest Hemingway: New Critical Essays.* Totowa, N.J.: Barnes & Noble, 1983.

Lewis, Robert W., Jr. "Hemingway in Italy: Making It Up." *Journal of Modern Literature* 9 (1982): 209–36.

———. *Hemingway On Love.* Austin: University of Texas Press, 1965.

Liedloff, Helmut. "Two War Novels: A Critical Comparison." *Revue de Littérature Comparée* 42 (1968): 390–406.

Light, James F. "The Religion of Death in *A Farewell to Arms*." *Modern Fiction Studies* 7 (1961): 169–73.

McCaffery, John K. M., ed. *Ernest Hemingway: The Man and His Work*. Cleveland: World Publishing, 1950.

McCarthy, Paul. "Chapter Beginnings in *A Farewell to Arms*." *Ball State University Forum* 10, no. 2 (1969): 21–30.

McIlvaine, Robert M. "A Literary Source for the Caesarean Section in *A Farewell to Arms*." *American Literature* 43 (1971): 444–47.

McNeely, Trevor. "War Zone Revisited: Hemingway's Aesthetics and *A Farewell to Arms*." *South Dakota Review* 22, no. 4 (1984): 14–38.

Marcus, Fred H. "*A Farewell to Arms*: The Impact of Irony and the Irrational." *The English Journal* 60 (1962): 527–35.

Mazzaro, Jerome L. "George Peele and *A Farewell to Arms*: A Thematic Tie?" *MLN* 75 (1960): 118–19.

Meyers, Jeffrey. *Hemingway: A Biography*. New York: Harper & Row, 1985.

———, ed. *Hemingway: The Critical Heritage*. London: Routledge & Kegan Paul, 1982.

Nagel, James, ed. *Ernest Hemingway: The Writer in Context*. Madison: University of Wisconsin Press, 1984.

Noble, Donald R., ed. *Hemingway: A Revaluation*. Troy, N.Y.: Whitston Publishing, 1983.

Nolan, Charles J., Jr. "Hemingway's Women's Movement." *Hemingway Review* 3, no. 2 (1984): 14–22.

———. "Shooting the Sergeant: Frederic Henry's Puzzling Action." *College Literature* 11, no. 3 (1984): 2–13.

Oldsey, Bernard. "The Genesis of *A Farewell to Arms*." *Studies in American Fiction* 5 (Autumn 1977): 175–85.

Reynolds, Michael S. *Hemingway's First War: The Making of* A Farewell to Arms. Princeton: Princeton University Press, 1976.

———. *Hemingway's Reading 1910–1940: An Inventory*. Princeton: Princeton University Press, 1976.

———. *The Young Hemingway*. Oxford: Basil Blackwell, 1986.

Rovit, Earl. *Ernest Hemingway*. New York: Twayne, 1963.

Russell, H. K. "The Catharsis in *A Farewell to Arms*." *Modern Fiction Studies* 1 (1955): 25–30.

Sharrock, Roger. "Singles and Couples: Hemingway's *A Farewell to Arms* and Updike's *Couples*." *Ariel* 4, no. 4 (1973): 21–43.

Simpson, Herbert. "The Problem of Structure in *A Farewell to Arms*." *Forum* (Houston) 4, no. 4 (1964): 20–24.

Smith, Paul. "Almost All is Vanity: A Note on Nine Rejected Titles for *A Farewell to Arms*." *Hemingway Review* 2, no. 1 (1982): 74–76.

Steinke, Jim. "Harlotry and Love: A Friendship in *A Farewell to Arms*." *Spectrum* 21, nos. 1–2 (1979): 20–24.

Stephens, Robert O. "Hemingway and Stendhal: The Matrix of *A Farewell to Arms*." *PMLA* 88 (1973): 271–79.

————. *Hemingway's Non-fiction: The Public Voice*. Chapel Hill: University of North Carolina Press, 1968.

Stubbs, John. "Love and Role-Playing in *A Farewell to Arms*." *Fitzgerald/Hemingway Annual* (1973): 237–44.

Toole, William B., III. "Religion, Love, and Nature in *A Farewell to Arms:* The Dark Shape of Irony." *CEA Critic* 29 (May 1967): 10–11.

Wagner, Linda W. *Ernest Hemingway: Five Decades of Criticism*. East Lansing: Michigan State University Press, 1974.

————. " 'Proud and Friendly and Gently': Women in Hemingway's Early Fiction." *College Literature* 7 (1980): 239–47.

Waldhorn, Arthur. *A Reader's Guide to Ernest Hemingway*. New York: Farrar, Straus & Giroux, 1972.

Weeks, Robert P., ed. *Hemingway: A Collection of Critical Essays*. Englewood Cliffs, N.J.: Prentice-Hall, 1962.

Wexler, Joyce. "E.R.A. for Hemingway: A Feminist Defense of *A Farewell to Arms*." *The Georgia Review* 35 (1981): 111–23.

White, William. "Hemingway in the Red Cross." *American Red Cross Journal* 42 (March 1966): 28–29.

Whitlow, Roger. *Cassandra's Daughters: The Women in Hemingway*. Westport, Conn.: Greenwood Press, 1984.

Williams, Wirt. *The Tragic Art of Ernest Hemingway*. Baton Rouge: Louisiana State University Press, 1981.

Wilson, Edmund. "Hemingway: Gauge of Morale." In *The Wound and the Bow*. Oxford: Oxford University Press, 1947.

Wylder, Delbert E. *Hemingway's Heroes*. Albuquerque: University of New Mexico Press, 1969.

Young, Philip. *Ernest Hemingway: A Reconsideration*. University Park: Pennsylvania State University Press, 1966.

Young, Philip, and Charles W. Mann, comps. *The Hemingway Manuscripts: An Inventory*. University Park: Pennsylvania State University Press, 1969.

Acknowledgments

"The Novel as Pure Poetry" (originally entitled "Hemingway's *A Farewell to Arms:* The Novel as Pure Poetry") by Daniel J. Schneider from *Modern Fiction Studies* 14, no. 3 (Autumn 1968), © 1968 by the Purdue Research Foundation, West Lafayette, Indiana. Reprinted by permission.

"Tragic Form in *A Farewell to Arms*" by Robert Merrill from *American Literature* 45, no. 4 (January 1974), © 1974 by Duke University Press. Reprinted by permission.

"*A Farewell to Arms*: A Dream Book" by William Adair from *The Journal of Narrative Technique* 5, no. 1 (January 1975), © 1975 by Eastern Michigan University Press. Reprinted by permission.

"Going Back" (originally entitled "Introduction: Going Back") by Michael S. Reynolds from *Hemingway's First War: The Making of* A Farewell to Arms by Michael S. Reynolds, © 1976 by Princeton University Press. Reprinted by permission of Princeton University Press.

"Hemingway's 'Resentful Cryptogram'" (originally entitled "*A Farewell to Arms:* Hemingway's 'Resentful Cryptogram'") by Judith Fetterley from *Journal of Popular Culture* 10, no. 1 (Summer 1976), © 1976 by Ray B. Browne. Reprinted by permission of the publisher.

"The Sense of an Ending in *A Farewell to Arms*" by Bernard Oldsey from *Modern Fiction Studies* 23, no. 4 (Winter 1977–78), © 1977 by the Purdue Research Foundation, West Lafayette, Indiana. Reprinted by permission.

"Frederic Henry's Escape and the Pose of Passivity" by Scott Donaldson from *Hemingway: A Revaluation,* edited by Donald R. Noble, © 1983 by Whitson Publishing Co. Reprinted by permission. The notes have been omitted.

"Pseudoautobiography and Personal Metaphor" (originally entitled "*A Farewell to Arms:* Pseudoautobiography and Personal Metaphor") by Millicent Bell from *Ernest Hemingway: The Writer in Context,* edited by James Nagel, © 1984 by the

Board of Regents of the University of Wisconsin System. Reprinted by permission of the University of Wisconsin Press.

"Catherine Barkley and the Hemingway Code: Ritual and Survival in *A Farewell to Arms*" by Sandra Whipple Spanier, © 1987 by Sandra Whipple Spanier. Published for the first time in this volume. Printed by permission.

Index

Adams, Nick (*In Our Time*), 38,
    44, 82, 97, 114, 135
Adventures of Huckleberry Finn
    (Twain), 1, 89
Algren, Nelson, 5
Anatomy of Criticism (Frye), 35
Anna Karenina (Tolstoy), 88
Antony and Cleopatra (Shakespeare),
    119
*Apprenticeship of Ernest Hemingway,
    The* (Fenton), 52
Aristotle, 25–26
Aspects of the Novel (Forster), 16, 87
Aymo, 27, 104, 109

Baker, Carlos, 29, 34, 50, 52, 57,
    72, 77–78, 82, 83, 124
Baker, Sheridan, 61, 97
Barkley, Catherine, 26, 81, 100; ag-
    gressiveness of, 69; as arche-
    type, 40; autonomy of, 134–
    35, 144, 146, 147–48; beauty
    of, 66; and betrayal, 70–72;
    biographical prototype for, 143;
    characterization of, 58–59; as
    code hero, 133–34, 135–36,
    137, 139, 145, 148; death of,
    5–6, 29, 63–64, 70, 78–79,
    108, 142–43; disillusionment
    of, 29–30, 136; and failure, 23–
    24; and fragmentation imagery,
    39; and Frederic Henry, 37, 68–

69, 101–2, 106–7, 147; and
    geometric imagery, 47; and
    hostile world, 138; humor of,
    136–37; idealization of, 131;
    objectification of, 17–18; pas-
    sivity of, 119, 120; point of
    view of, 119; pregnancy of,
    18, 28, 68; prescience of, 138–
    39, 146–47; and rain symbol,
    18; as realist, 138; and respon-
    sibility, 69–70; and romance,
    45; and spatial imagery, 73, 74;
    as statue, 24, 84, 85, 93; sto-
    icism of, 137; submergence in
    relationship of, 110, 134, 140–
    41
Barnes, Jake (*The Sun Also Rises*),
    38
Barth, John, 92
Bell, Millicent, 131, 137
Belloc, Hilaire, 58
Benson, Jackson J., 67–68, 134
Bloom, Molly (*Ulysses*), 89
Bonello, 84, 104, 109, 121
Bourne, Catherine (*The Garden of
    Eden*), 144–45
Bourne, David (*The Garden of
    Eden*), 144
Boyle, Kay, 143
Brady, Matthew, 54
Brontë, Charlotte, 131, 146
Brontë, Emily, 17
Brooks, Van Wyck, 10, 58

Burke, Kenneth, 85, 93

Canby, H. S., 50
Cantwell, Colonel (*Across the River and into the Trees*), 38, 44, 139
Cézanne, Paul, 13, 41, 45
Conrad, Joseph, 7
Cowley, Malcolm, 6, 33, 50, 52
Crane, Stephen, 54–55, 118
Crime and Punishment (Dostoevsky), 89

Dedalus, Stephen (*Ulysses*), 30
Dekker, George, 138
Donaldson, Scott, 142
Dorman-Smith, Captain E. E., 54
Dos Passos, John, 58
Dostoevsky, Fyodor, 89

Earnshaw, Catherine (*Wuthering Heights*), 17
Eliot, George, 87
Eliot, T. S., 6, 16
Emilio, 101, 102–3, 104, 106
Erikson, Erik, 72
Ernest Hemingway: Critiques of Four Major Novels (Baker), 78
Ettore, 18, 83–84, 120, 136
Existence and Being (Heidegger), 90

Farewell to Arms, A: affective failure in, 117–19; as apologia, 111; as autobiographical novel, 52, 57–59, 113–17, 123–29; bitterness in, 10–11, 19–20; characterization in, 15–16, 25, 29; character of love affair in, 66–72, 119–20, 134–35, 137; conclusion of, 77–87, 92–96, 116, 129, 142–43; conversation in, 17; criticism of, 50–52, 131–32, 139–42, 147; cyclical structure in, 28; darkness as symbol in, 36–37, 45–46, 82–83, 86–87; death in, 63–64, 79–80, 122–23; death of baby in, 64, 81–82, 122; dreamlike qualities of, 33–48; emotional contrasts in, 12, 18, 22–23, 24; fox image in, 111–12, 123; fragmentation imagery in, 38–40, 42–43, 46; geometric structure of, 34–35, 39, 43; hallway imagery in, 46–47; hostile world in, 26–28, 31, 71; hostility toward women in, 6, 62–75, 142; images of failure in, 13, 14, 23–24; lack of plot in, 117; limitations of, 4–5, 108; love as religion in, 17, 18, 23, 31; as lyric novel, 10, 35, 43; male culture in, 62–63; manuscript versions of, 58, 77–85, 94–96, 100, 127, 132, 142, 145–46; motif of disguise in, 61; nihilism in, 80, 85, 92; as novel of education, 132–33; objectivity in, 117–18; omens in, 28–29, 36; opening of, 7–8; paradigm of action in, 37–38, 42, 46; passage of time in, 37, 42; passion for immediacy in, 8; passive voice in, 14; as personal exorcism, 35; plot in, 12; rain symbol in, 6, 12–13, 14, 18–20, 21–22, 23, 28, 79, 84; realism of, 50–52, 55–56, 115; religion in, 81, 85, 128; repetition in, 20–21, 43, 46–47; romance with Europe in, 5; romantic elements in, 34, 40–42, 45, 61; seasons as symbolic in, 36, 37, 40, 41, 44, 45; sex and death in, 35–36, 45, 74; sexuality in, 62–63, 106–7; snow image in, 23; spatial imagery in, 72–74; statue image in, 24, 84, 85, 93; symbolism of despair in, 12–15; time in, 92; title of, 132; as tragedy, 25–32, 142; under-

statement in, 4, 85; war in, 27, 115, 137–38
Fathers and Sons (Turgenev), 89
Fenton, Charles, 52, 57
Ferguson, Miss, 67, 111
Fetterley, Judith, 131, 142, 147
Fiedler, Leslie, 5, 142
Fielding, Henry, 88
Fischer, Doc ("God Rest You Merry, Gentlemen"), 3
Fitzgerald, F. Scott, 58–59, 80–81, 139
Flaubert, Gustave, 88
Fleming, Henry (*The Red Badge of Courage*), 118
Ford, Ford Madox, 55
Forster, E. M., 16, 87, 89, 93
Freud, Sigmund, 35, 38
Frye, Northrop, 35

Gellhorn, Martha, 144
George, 40–41, 45
Gilligan, Carol, 141–42
Gino, 26, 118, 129
Grapes of Wrath, The (Steinbeck), 89
Grebstein, Sheldon Norman, 100
Greene, Gayle, 147
Greffi, Count, 23, 106, 133; and love as religion, 31, 128, 140; as mentor, 81, 104, 122
Gurko, Leo, 131
Guttingen, Mr. and Mrs., 45

Hackett, Frances, 131
Harris, Joseph, 138
Heidegger, Martin, 90, 91
Hemingway, Dr. Clarence, 124
Hemingway, Ernest: on *Across the River and into the Trees,* 34; on *A Farewell to Arms,* 25; androgyny of, 141; and biography, 57; and Cézanne, 13, 41, 45; code of, 132, 134, 135–36, 137–38, 139; and Conrad, 7; and Crane, 54–55; and Emersonian tradition, 3; and fear, 110; and Fitzgerald, 59, 80–81; and geography, 50; hostility toward women of, 6; influences on, 1–3; as journalist, 55; and Keats, 8; and Kipling, 1; and marriage, 123, 127; on memory, 56; objectivity of, 56; personal life of, 123–26; as poet, 2; public image of, 5, 52, 143; realistic style of, 114–15; sexuality of, 125–26, 141; as short-story writer, 3–5; and Stevens, 2; on subject matter, 48; tragic vision of, 142; and Twain, 1; war experience of, 49–50, 113; and Whitman, 1–2; wounding of, 35, 114; writing methods of, 52–54, 77–78, 84, 85–86. *Works: Across the River and into the Trees,* 34; "Big Two-Hearted River," 33, 52–53, 85, 135; "Cat in the Rain," 57; "A Clean, Well-Lighted Place," 80, 82, 90–91, 92; *Death in the Afternoon,* 142, 145, 148; "The Doctor and the Doctor's Wife," 125; *The First Forty-Nine Stories,* 2; *For Whom the Bell Tolls,* 4, 97; *The Garden of Eden,* 132, 141, 144–45; "God Rest You Merry, Gentlemen," 3; *Green Hills of Africa,* 56; "In Another Country," 126–27; "Indian Camp," 114, 124; *In Our Time,* 38, 54, 97, 124; *Men at War,* 54; *Men without Women,* 126; *A Moveable Feast,* 50, 56; "My Old Man," 114; "A Natural History of the Dead," 3, 38; "Now I Lay Me," 33, 82, 114, 126, 127; *The Old Man and the Sea,* 92; "The Snows of Kilimanjaro," 23; *To Have and Have Not,* 4; "The Torrents of Spring," 58;

Hemingway, Ernest (*continued*)
"A Veteran Visits Old Front,"
49; "A Way You'll Never Be,"
33, 44, 82; *Winner Take Nothing,* 92. See also *A Farewell to Arms; The Sun Also Rises*
Hemingway, Mary, 50
Hemingway's fiction: autobiographical nature of, 53; characterization in, 11–12; darkness as symbol in, 82; dreamlike quality of, 33; food and drink in, 12; hostile world in, 10, 137–38; images of death in, 38; marriage in, 126–27; nihilism in, 90–92; objectivity in, 16; pattern of education in, 132–33; as personal exorcism, 35; plot in, 12; purity of, 9–12; relationships in, 6; symbolism in, 11; syntax in, 115; understatement in, 4, 10, 85–86, 126, 145; women in, 131, 132; wound image in, 33
Hemingway's First War (Reynolds), 82
Henry, Frederic, 6, 26, 99, 101; affective failure of, 117–18, 120–22, 128; apathy of, 127–28; as archetype, 40; as autobiographical character, 108, 114; and betrayal, 71–72; blindness of, 134–35, 146–47; capacity for love of, 110; characterization of, 58–59, 139; and darkness symbol, 82–83, 86–87; dependence of, 137; depression of, 16–17, 21; and desertion, 103; deviousness of, 101–3, 111–12; disillusionment of, 29–30, 36; education of, 137, 138–39, 148; egotism of, 67–69, 72; fear of death of, 38; and fragmentation imagery, 39, 42–43; and geometric imagery, 39, 43; guilt of, 98, 100, 101, 103, 104–8, 111; and hallway imagery, 47;

Hemingway's distance from, 108–10, 111; hostility to women of, 64–66, 74–75; incompetence of, 109; and life as tragedy, 26–27; and love as religion, 18, 30–31, 118–19; and marriage, 136; and Miss Van Campen, 65–66; as moral policeman, 103–4; and nihilism, 80; passivity of, 69–70, 97–98, 111, 119, 145–46; point of view of, 64, 79, 108; pragmatism of, 138, 142; purification of, 17, 18; responsibility of, 97; and romance, 45; sense of loss of, 8, 128–29; separateness from male culture of, 64; sickness of, 72; and spatial imagery, 73–74; and understatement, 86; and war, 122; wounding of, 36, 79, 114
Hergesheimer, Joseph, 58
Hickok, Guy, 58
Hovey, Ricard B., 68, 141
Hutchinson, Percy, 50

In a Different Voice: Psychological Theory and Women's Development (Gilligan), 141–42

James, Henry, 58, 87, 90, 94
Jaspers, Karl, 111
Jew of Malta, The (Marlowe), 126
Jordan, Robert (*For Whom the Bell Tolls*), 97
Joyce, James, 11–12, 30, 89

Kafka, Franz, 34, 41, 48
Kahn, Coppélia, 147
Keats, John, 8
Kermode, Frank, 87–88, 89, 90
Killinger, John, 70
Kim (Kipling), 1
Kipling, Rudyard, 1

Lewis, Robert, 70–71
Lewis, Wyndham, 6–7, 69
Light, James, 140
Lost in the Funhouse (Barth), 92
Love Story (Segal), 61

Madame Bovary (Flaubert), 88
Mailer, Norman, 3
Making a Difference: Feminist Literary Criticism (Greene and Kahn), 147
Mann, Charles, 78
Marlowe, Christopher, 126
Martz, Louis L., 6
Melville, Herman, 34
Merimée, Prosper, 6–7
Meyers, 40
Mippipopolous, Count (*The Sun Also Rises*), 122
Miss Lonelyhearts (West), 3
Morrison, Toni, 147
Mulligan, Buck (*Ulysses*), 11–12
Munich, Adrienne, 147

Novel, the: as autobiography, 113, 123; conclusion of, 87–90, 93, 94

"Ode on Melancholy" (Keats), 8
O'Hara, John, 5
Oldsey, Bernard, 142–43
Othello (Shakespeare), 64

Passini, 27, 30
Pater, Walter, 6–7, 8
Perkins, Maxwell, 57, 58, 108, 125
Pfeiffer, Pauline, 115, 123, 144
Piani, 84, 104
Pierre (Melville), 34
Plimpton, George, 78, 142
Poe, Edgar Allan, 11
Poetics (Aristotle), 26
Priest, the, 18, 83, 115–16; discouragement of, 27, 120; and ideal of service, 128, 138, 140; and symbolism of despair, 15–16; wisdom of, 81, 118, 129, 133
Pynchon, Thomas, 3

Red Badge of Courage, The (Crane), 54, 118
Reynolds, Michael S., 82, 100, 127–28, 139
Richardson, Hadley, 115, 144
Rinaldi, 18, 83, 98, 109, 115–16, 118; contempt for women of, 62–63, 71–72; depression of, 27, 29, 120; and desertion, 103; and fragmentation imagery, 42; and love as religion, 120, 137; as mentor, 81, 129, 133; and sense of failure, 21, 33; and sense of pollution, 16, 21; and sexuality, 64
Robbe-Grillet, Alain, 34
Romeo and Juliet (Shakespeare), 119
Rose of Sharon (*The Grapes of Wrath*), 89
Ross, Lillian, 13
Rossi, Alberto, 52
Rovit, Earl, 44, 139–40

Santiago (*The Old Man and the Sea*), 92
Schneider, Daniel, 140–41
Schorer, Mark, 84
Scribner, Charles, 125
Segal, Erich, 61
Sense of an Ending, The (Kermode), 87–88
Sexuality: in Hemingway's life, 124, 125–26; and hostility towards women, 62–63, 64; as narcotic, 106–7
Shakespeare, William, 64, 119
Shirley (C. Brontë), 131, 146
Shrike (*Miss Lonelyhearts*), 3
Simmons, 83, 100–101, 104
Smith, Julian, 126

Sophocles, 32
Stein, Gertrude, 54, 56
Steinbeck, John, 89
Stevens, Wallace, 2
Strater, Mike, 54
Strindberg, August, 34
Sun Also Rises, The, 2, 4, 124; bio-
    graphical prototypes in, 57, 58;
    dreamlike quality of, 33; emo-
    tional contrasts in, 24; plot in,
    12

Tender Is the Night (Fitzgerald), 80
Thackeray, William, 88
"To His Coy Mistress" (Marvell),
    28, 68
Tolstoy, Leo, 88
Tom Jones (Fielding), 88
Turgenev, Ivan, 89
Twain, Mark, 1, 89

Ulysses (Joyce), 11–12, 30, 89

Valentini, Dr., 40, 133
Van Campen, Miss, 19, 64, 65, 103
Vanity Fair (Thackeray), 88
von Kurowsky, Agnes, 115, 143–44

Wagner, Linda, 132
Walker, Mrs., 66
War and Peace (Tolstoy), 88
Warren, Robert Penn, 2, 4, 6, 9, 10
Waste Land, The (Eliot), 16
Welsh, Mary, 144
Wescott, Glenway, 58
West, Nathanael, 3
Wexler, Joyce, 132, 134, 147
Whitman, Walt, 1–2, 6
Wilson, Edmund, 131
Wister, Owen, 108
Wuthering Heights (E. Brontë), 17

Young, Philip, 35, 52, 57, 78, 131,
    138, 139